PRAYING WITH JESUS

MEDITATIONS ON THE LORD'S PRAYER

MICHAEL LODAHL

THE FOUNDRY
PUBLISHING®

Cover design: J.R. Caines
Interior design: Sharon Page

Library of Congress Cataloging-in-Publication Data
Names: Lodahl, Michael E., 1955- author.
Title: Praying with Jesus : meditations on the Lord's prayer / Michael Lodahl.
Description: Kansas City, MO : The Foundry Publishing, [2022] | Includes bibliographical references.
    | Summary: "In Praying with Jesus, Michael Lodahl breaks down the Lord's Prayer line by line, infusing fresh meaning into the ancient words. The added biblical context, theological background, and cultural understanding will bring new life to our corporate recitations of this well-known prayer, and help readers discover the power and purpose behind it"— Provided by publisher.
Identifiers: LCCN 2021046100 (print) | LCCN 2021046101 (ebook) | ISBN 9780834139206 | ISBN 9780834139213 (ebook)
Subjects: LCSH: Lord's prayer—Meditations.
Classification: LCC BV230 .L53 2022 (print) | LCC BV230 (ebook) | DDC 226.9/606—dc23
LC record available at https://lccn.loc.gov/2021046100
LC ebook record available at https://lccn.loc.gov/2021046101

10 9 8 7 6 5 4 3 2 1

CONTENTS

PREFACE

This little book grew out of a sermon series I first preached a few years ago when I served as the interim pastor for Hemet Church of the Nazarene in southern California. During my extended time there, I incorporated the Lord's Prayer as a regular part of the congregation's Sunday morning worship service. Of course, for many Christian congregations this is a given; for many others, however, praying the Lord's Prayer together is rare.

None of the congregants at my interim church complained—at least as far as I knew! But I did fear that some might wonder why we regularly engaged this formulaic and formalized prayer—something we normally leave to Catholics and Episcopalians and such. So it seemed a good idea to devote some sermonic attention to this prayer that Jesus himself taught to his disciples. It was a prayer I learned as a boy, probably in Sunday school, possibly Vacation Bible School, but it was also a prayer we simply did not pray in typical Sunday worship services as I grew up in evangelical congregations in eastern Washington. If I was so intent on changing that practice among these good-hearted folk in California, shouldn't I have a reason? And so a sermon series was born.

Along with occasional stints as an interim pastor, I have been blessed in the past few years with the opportunity to preach often as part-time teaching pastor at St. Timothy Lutheran Church in San Diego. This church has been a warm and tremendously supportive congregation to my wife, Janice, and me, and it has also been a great friend to Point Loma Nazarene University, where I teach theology. These lovely Lutherans pray the Lord's Prayer together every Sunday, so it seemed like a good idea to walk with them as well, sermon by sermon, phrase by phrase, through the prayer. With them, the question would be less about why we were praying the prayer but more like: What is it, exactly, that we've been praying all these years?

I am deeply grateful to the warmhearted, saintly folks in both congregations whose active listening and encouraging responses have made preaching the gospel in their midst a real joy. Thank you, friends. These meditations are dedicated to all of you.

THE LORD'S PRAYER

Our Father, who art in heaven
Hallowed be your name.
Your kingdom come, your will be done
On earth as it is in heaven.
Give us this day our daily bread.
And forgive us our trespasses
As we forgive those who trespass against us.
And lead us not into temptation,
But deliver us from evil.
For yours is the kingdom and
the power and the glory forever.
Amen

WHY WE SHOULD
PRAY THIS PRAYER

———— •◆• ————

Many Christians pray the Lord's Prayer every Sunday in church. Among those for whom this prayer is a regular, corporate practice we'd find Roman Catholics, Episcopalians, Lutherans, Presbyterians, United Methodists, and many others. Most churches that are more likely to be described as evangelical tend to pray this prayer together less often, perhaps especially if they are non-denominational, charismatic, or Pentecostal. So it was in the churches where I grew up.

Things are definitely changing, but many Christians from Holiness traditions have historically looked skeptically at anything in church that seems too ritualistic. Memorized prayers that we recite together? Shouldn't prayer be spontaneous? Shouldn't we just pray from the heart? Doesn't a memorized prayer recited together seem a little too, well, 'Catholic'? That's the way many have viewed the matter.

Granted, even churches that tend to emphasize and celebrate the spontaneity of worship in the presence and power of the Holy Spirit—believers such as Pentecostals, charismatics, and Holiness folk—usually (perhaps inevitably) have their own rituals in worship. Often, there ends up being a fairly predictable order of worship from Sunday to Sunday, even if there is no bulletin that would make this order or pattern obvious. The rituals and patterns may go relatively unnoticed and generally unannounced. Nonetheless, it turns out that even spontaneity can become scripted. Humans are creatures of habit. Christians are humans. The key, of course, is to develop the right habits.

Certainly it is debatable whether Jesus intended this prayer to be a ritual performed in the exact same way every time; it is possible he offered it as a model or general example of what and how to pray. Further, Scripture assures us that empty rituals are not what God desires. God longs to hear the cries of our hearts in prayer. But there is no need for a prayer like the Lord's Prayer to *be* an empty ritual; it all depends on how we pray it. Ritual can help shape and guide our hearts, our emotions, our longings for God. It can give us words—tested and tried over centuries of use—when our own words seem to fail us.

But that probably wasn't the deepest concern with the Lord's Prayer. The fact is, a lot of Holiness Christians used to get nervous about a specific part of this prayer. We'll have more to say on this later in the book, but let me drop this hint that some Christians haven't always been confident that Jesus was doing the right thing to encourage us to pray, "Forgive us our trespasses as we forgive those who trespass against us." That seems a little defeatist, you know? Holiness Christians historically have been about living sanctified (holy) lives, and how are you going to encourage holy lives if people expect that they're always going to have some sin, or even a batch of sins, to confess? Holiness is about being freed from sin, not acting like you're always going to have something that needs to be forgiven. Granted, there are considerable problems with this mentality, but I'll save it for later.

There is one other preliminary matter. To be honest, I was pleasantly surprised when Bonnie Perry, the editorial director at The Foundry Publishing, went along with my proposed title, apparently without the slightest hesitation. *Praying with Jesus?* I thought there might be some question about that; after all, when we pray, are we praying *with* Jesus? Does Jesus pray? The Gospels inform us that he *prayed*, but would it be correct to say he still does? And is it presumptuous for us to say we pray along with him?

Perhaps such questions do not particularly bother you, but just in case, I want to address them a little. First of all, it is clear that Jesus certainly *was* a person of deep prayer life. That comes to the fore especially in the Gospel of Luke, where Jesus is described as praying quite a lot more than in the other Gospels. It is also the Gospel in which Jesus teaches us about praying a lot more than the other Gospels. So I think it's safe to assume that Luke was interested in the act and discipline of prayer, and desired his readers to appreciate that Jesus was a person of prayer. In fact, in Luke 11 we read that Jesus's disciples appear to witness him praying right before they ask him to teach them how to do it too: "Lord, teach us to pray, just as John taught his disciples" (v. 1). Among the Synoptic Gospels (Matthew, Mark, Luke), the Gospel of Mark doesn't have a Lord's Prayer narrative, and Matthew's version doesn't say that Jesus is praying right before it happens;

instead, Jesus includes the Lord's Prayer as part of his Sermon on the Mount (Matthew 5–7). There are several other instances like this in Luke, where a common story shared among the three Synoptic Gospels includes only in Luke the rather significant detail that Jesus is praying (Jesus's baptism in Luke 3:21 and his transfiguration in 9:29 are two such examples).

Although the global church and our general approach in this book works with Matthew's version most often, we should at least mention that Luke's version of the prayer is noticeably briefer. Even so, Luke's Gospel as a whole definitely has far more to say about praying! Some of our most fascinating observations about the Gospels arise from the process of comparing them with one another. By virtue of such comparison, we may come to appreciate the heightened emphasis that Luke places on Jesus's own prayer life.

Beyond the Gospels, however, the New Testament teaches us not only that Jesus *was* a man of prayer but that, in fact, he still is. Two passages in particular suggest this fact to us. In Romans 8, Paul becomes blessedly overwhelmed by the reality of God's love and proclaims to his readers, "If God is for us, who can be against us? He who did not spare his own Son, but gave him up for us all— how will he not also, along with him, graciously give us all things? Who will bring any charge against those whom God has chosen? It is God who justifies. Who then is the one who condemns? No one. [After all,] Christ Jesus who died—more than that, who was raised to life—is at the right hand of God and is also interceding for us" (vv. 31b–34). Jesus is interceding for us! Like, right now! When you intercede for someone, you pray for them, speaking to God on their behalf. Paul proclaims that Jesus, the one who "lives to God"

(Romans 6:10) is, in this present moment, speaking to God on our behalf. Surely that qualifies as prayer.

The book of Hebrews makes the same point in perhaps even more dramatic fashion. Jesus is called "a priest forever" (7:21). Consequently, "because Jesus lives forever, he has a permanent priesthood. Therefore he is able to save completely those who come to God through him, because he always lives to intercede for them" (vv. 24–25). Always and forever, Jesus intercedes. If we were to wonder what Jesus might say in those unending prayers of intercession, a worthy suggestion that I learned from my Sunday school teacher Reuben Welch is that he has not veered terribly far from the kinds of things we read in John 17:

> *Holy Father, protect them by the power of your name, the name you gave me, so that they may be one as we are one. (v. 11b)*

> *Sanctify them by the truth; your word is truth. (v. 17)*

> *That all of them may be one, Father, just as you are in me and I am in you. May they also be in us, so that the world may believe that you have sent me. (v. 21)*

This prayer from John 17 is traditionally called Jesus's "high priestly prayer," and the Gospel of John strongly implies that Jesus is still praying it today. For that matter, it does not seem a stretch at all to imagine that Jesus still prays the prayer he taught his own disciples to pray. So when *we* pray, yes, I think there is a profound sense in which we can be assured that we are praying with Jesus.

But I'm still thinking about those Christians from my childhood who got nervous about ritual. I think perhaps they overlooked how often our lives are governed by ritualized language:

> *Good morning!*
> *Please.*
> *Thank you.*
> *Excuse me.*
> *I'm sorry.*
> *With this ring I thee wed.*
> *Bless you!* (after a sneeze, naturally).
> *Ashes to ashes, and dust to dust.*
> *I'm not interested.*
> And my favorite: *Yes, I'll hold.*

None of us invents the language(s) we speak; further, our culture in a great many instances teaches us how to use the language it has given us. Cultural rituals teach us to speak meaningfully to one another. It's certainly also true that ritual language can become formal and stilted, but it need not. Really, we try to teach our children to employ ritual language, but we also insist that it be genuine. How many times have parents insisted to children that they must apologize to their siblings or their friends "like you *mean* it"? Surely we can say it like we mean it when it comes to praying the prayer Jesus taught his disciples to pray.

What I hope to do in the following meditations is to help us know what we mean when we pray this prayer, precisely so that we *can* pray it like we mean it.

And so, let us pray.

☙ 1 ❧
OUR FATHER

Our Father, who art in heaven
Hallowed be your name

"Our"

"Our." It's called the first-person-plural possessive. Jesus teaches that we are never to pray for show, never to impress other people with our spiritual eloquence. In fact, he says we should pray privately behind closed doors (Matthew 6:6). *And yet*—even when we enter into that intimate space of communion with God, Jesus instructs us to say, "*Our* Father." No matter when or where you pray, you are never praying alone! John Wesley famously said "there is no holiness but social holiness" because we are members of the body of Christ. If Wesley was right about that, then in a very important sense there is also no prayer but social prayer. Because we pray as a people, even when we pray alone, we are incorporated together as a people into the beauty of Jesus's relationship to his Father.

Later in the Gospel of Matthew we read of Jesus praying, "I praise you, Father, Lord of heaven and earth, because you have hidden these things from the wise and learned, and revealed them to little children" (11:25). Then, abruptly, Jesus interrupts his own prayer (or does he?) by turning to us: "Come to me, all you who are weary and burdened, and I will give you rest" (v. 28). Notice that in this passage Jesus essentially invites us into his prayer life, into the intimacy and honesty of his relationship with his Father.

We recall Jesus's baptism, where Matthew tells us that at the very moment he came up from the Jordan River, "heaven was opened, and he saw the Spirit of God descending like a dove and alighting on him. And a voice from heaven said, 'This is my Son, whom I love; with him I am well pleased'" (3:16b–17). Accordingly, when we are baptized, we are baptized into Christ, such that we are drawn into the very life—including the prayer life—of God's faithful Son (Romans 6:3–11).

Recall, too, what Jesus teaches us about family. Later in Matthew we read:

> While Jesus was still talking to the crowd, his mother and brothers stood outside, wanting to speak to him. Someone told him, "Your mother and your brothers are standing outside, wanting to speak to you." He replied to him, "Who is my mother, and who are my brothers?" Pointing to his disciples, he said, "Here are my mother and my brothers. For whoever does the will of my Father"—notice that Jesus *can* say "my Father"—"in heaven is my brother and sister and mother." (12:46–50)

We've become family—to Jesus! And because of Jesus and in Jesus's name, we are invited to pray to *our* Father.

I think, finally, of the nature of Jesus's rule—or leadership style, we might call it. In Matthew 23, Jesus contrasts his ways with the ways of the scribes and Pharisees:

> They love the place of honor at banquets and the most important seats in the synagogues; they love to be greeted with respect in the marketplaces and to be called 'Rabbi' by others. But you are not to be called 'Rabbi,' for you have one Teacher, and you are all [siblings]. And do not call anyone on earth 'father,' for you have one Father, and he is in heaven." (vv. 6–9).

It is important to remember that in the Greek it's "*y'all* have one Father"—the way they say it down South. He is speaking to a group here, not to people as individuals. "Y'all together have one Father," and that is why Jesus teaches us to pray, even when we pray alone, to *our* Father. In actual fact, we are never alone!

Now, all this does not mean there is never a place for individualized language ("me" or "my") in our prayers. But it really should never be the primary language we use, for the body of Christ precedes each of us through many generations of disciples who have prayed this prayer (and many other prayers!) well before us, in many different languages. And when we pray today, we join millions of other Christians around the world who lift up their hearts in this very prayer. Theologian Marjorie Hewitt Suchocki recounts her experiences of praying the Lord's Prayer in foreign places, alongside fellow believers who prayed in a different language:

*Each one of us is enfolded into
this great family, this organic,
living unity that is Christ's body.
We pray together with all
of our fellow disciples.*

When the time comes in the service for the people to unite in the cadence of this particular prayer, I know I am at home in the Spirit of Christ. As I softly join in the prayer with my foreigner's tongue, I know that the language of the prayer uniting us is deeper than the differences of speech that otherwise separate us. The Lord's Prayer is itself an ever-living creation of unity akin to the unity manifested in that great high priestly prayer recorded in John 17.[1]

Each one of us is enfolded into this great family, this organic, living unity that is Christ's body. We pray together with all of our fellow disciples. Even so, I mentioned briefly already that within this beautiful reality called church, there is yet a place for you and me to say "me" and "mine" and "I" in our praying. Allow me to illustrate this profound truth with a marvelous song of David from that Jewish hymnal we call the Psalms. In Psalm 139, David prays:

*You have searched me, L*ORD*, and you know me. (v. 1)*

How precious to me are your thoughts, God! How vast is the sum of them! (v. 17)

If only you, God, would slay the wicked! Away from me, you who are bloodthirsty! (v. 19)

---

1. Marjorie Hewitt Suchocki, *In God's Presence: Theological Reflections on Prayer* (St. Louis, MO: Chalice Press, 1996), 104.

Do I not hate those who hate you, LORD, and abhor those who are in rebellion against you? I have nothing but hatred for them; I count them my enemies. (vv. 21–22)

Search me, God, and know my heart; test me and know my anxious thoughts. (v. 23)

It is obvious that David is praying things here that are not encouraged in the prayer Jesus teaches his disciples! He is understandably bothered by the presence of evildoers in the world. David is doing some serious ranting here, getting increasingly revved up. He is engaging in the art of projection at its very best (or worst!): *all the evil is out there in those people, and God hates them as much as I do!* Indeed, this might well be the nasty underside to all the positive values we have identified in the communal nature of the Lord's Prayer. *We're God's people, so they're not.* They're the bad people, which must mean we're the good people, right? They're evil, so we must be righteous. God is on our side, and most definitely not on theirs. May they experience God's damnation—and right soon!

Then something happens in this prayer of David that seems a lot like a miracle: *Search **me**, God, and know **my** heart.* Suddenly, it seems that—presumably by the prompting presence of the Holy Spirit—David changes his tune. He moves from self-righteous, angry projection upon all those evildoers *out there* and allows the divine searchlight to interrogate *him. Try me, examine me, I pray, and know **my** thoughts.* How much easier it is to assume the problem lies with those evil people who are not part of my people! But David, by the grace of God, continues his prayer in a much more painfully probing attitude: "See if there is any wicked way in *me*" (v. 24, NRSV). Granted, this conclusion to Psalm 139 is not part of the prayer Jesus teaches his disciples, but it is arguable that it anticipates what Jesus teaches about forgiveness in his prayer: *forgive us our trespasses as we forgive those who trespass against us.*

Further, it is a marvelous example of individualized prayer. *Search **me**, God.* Even here, of course, David's prayer is offered up from within the historical, social, and religious context of his community—the people Israel. Thus, even his radically self-searching, individual prayer is also communal prayer; indeed, the fact that it is part of the Jewish hymnal (you can hear this prayer still being prayed today in synagogues around the world)—a psalm prayed by millions of Jews and Christians through the centuries—underscores its communal dimension. Thus, Christians who pray this prayer of David, offering it to the God of Israel in the name of Jesus Christ, never pray it alone. They pray it as members of the universal body of Christ that thrives not only in the present but also down through the centuries since Jesus taught his disciples how they should pray.

"Father"

For a considerable number of Christians today, the designation of "Father" for God is not particularly happy or welcome. Usually their hesitation involves personal experiences or the experiences of people they care about with fathers who were distant, authoritarian, absent, abusive, or some combination thereof. For such people, the term "father" is not a source of comfort but of pain or even terror. Love for our neighbor demands that such concerns not be dismissed.

It should not surprise or disturb us, then, to learn that some people find maternal imagery for God to be more inviting, and we should also recognize that female metaphors for God are not lacking in the Bible (see Deuteronomy 32:18; Matthew 23:37; Luke 15:8–10). But, of course, not all moms have been good and loving parents either; thus, the same challenge applies. The real issue, finally, is the extent to which any of our designations for God is adequate for the Holy One who dwells infinitely beyond all human experience, language, and thought. "God is not a human being" (Numbers 23:19), and if that is the case, then it seems unavoidable to admit that God is neither male nor female. God exists infinitely beyond creaturely sexual differentiation. This truth should never be forgotten when we pray to the Creator of all things by saying, "Our Father."

Yet we should remember, too, what we find in the very opening of our Bibles: God created humanity (Hebrew, *adam*) in the divine image *as male and female*. So, even though God is neither male nor female, all human beings share in God's image, in God's calling upon all people to reflect God's character like a face in a mirror. Each and every human being is created and called to be God's likeness.[2] If great Christian theologians like Thomas Aquinas and John Wesley are correct, then everything that God creates shares, to some extent, in the nature and mind of the Creator; otherwise, they could not have been created! How much more is this the case with human beings, the only creatures the Bible describes as having been made *in God's image*? Given the fact that male and female both, and equally, share in this honor of being created in God's image, of having

---

2. See Michael Lodahl and April Cordero, *Renewal in Love: Living Holy Lives in God's Good Creation* (Kansas City, MO: Beacon Hill Press of Kansas City, 2014), especially 29–44.

God exists infinitely beyond creaturely sexual differentiation. This truth should never be forgotten when we pray to the Creator of all things by saying, "Our Father."

been "crowned with glory and honor" (Psalm 8:5) by their Creator, then women's existence (like men's) is rooted deeply in the very nature of God. Accordingly, it should not surprise us that in the song of Moses we read Moses's lament to the people of Israel, "You were unmindful of the Rock that bore you; you forgot the God who gave you birth" (Deuteronomy 32:18). Of course, God is not literally a rock, and God has not literally given birth to the nation of Israel. But neither is God literally a father. The language is symbolic and deeply meaningful, but it does not and cannot capture *who and what God is*. Accordingly, the designation "Father" does not and cannot exhaust the riches of God's infinitely vast and unspeakably deep being.

To all this, some may object by pointing out that Jesus's favored designation for God is "Father." New Testament scholars generally assume that Jesus's practice is to call God *Abba*, an Aramaic term of intimacy that is still used among Hebrew-speaking people today. While perhaps that sense of intimacy has been overdramatized at times, it does appear to correspond most closely, in English, to "Papa" or "DaDa." It is noteworthy that in our four Gospels, the Aramaic *Abba* appears only once—in Mark's description of Jesus praying in the garden of Gethsemane (14:36)—but there are good reasons to assume it was Jesus's regular practice. Interestingly, in passages from two of his letters, we read of Paul characterizing Christian prayer—especially since it is prayer empowered by the Holy Spirit—as "Abba! Father!" just as we find in Gethsemane (Romans 8:15–16; Galatians 4:6).

There is no question, then, that Jesus calls upon God as his *Abba*, and that he emboldens his followers to imitate his practice. This does not mean God is a white-bearded man in the clouds, nor even that God is a male spirit of some kind. Indeed, this is a false teaching. Let us recall again that "God is not a human being" and, if not a human being (or any other creature), then not male. But if that is true, then what does it mean when we pray, "Our *Father*"?

Probably the best way to address this question is to examine the kinds of things Jesus says about God as Father. Here are some of the most pertinent examples from the Gospel of Matthew:

God the Father loves all people (5:43–48).

God the Father "sees in secret" what is "done in secret" and knows what we need before we ask (6:1–6, 7).

God the Father is a forgiving God but also expects us to be forgiving (18:35).

God the Father feeds the birds of the air (6:26).

Not even a sparrow falls to the ground apart from our Father's knowledge and compassion (10:29).

When we address God as "Father," we are confessing this particular rendering of God that Jesus has shared with us. And what sort of father is this? Authoritarian? Aloof? Abusive? Hardly! Roman Catholic theologian Elizabeth Johnson writes that, in Jesus's understanding, "*Abba* is the very opposite of a dominating patriarch. Rather, this compassionate, intimate, and close *Abba* releases everyone from patterns of domination and calls for anoth-

*The problem is not that
God is called "Father"
but that more fathers
are not like God.*

er kind of community."[3] Indeed, Jesus even occasionally compares human parents to God as our Father, and not surprisingly, God comes out ahead: "If you, then, though you are evil, know how to give good gifts to your children, how much more will your Father in heaven give good gifts to those who ask him!" (Matthew 7:11).

We hear even more dramatic language from the prophet Isaiah: "Can a woman forget her nursing child, or show no compassion for the child of her womb? Even these may forget, yet I will not forget you. See, I have inscribed you on the palms of my hands; your walls are continually before me" (49:15–16, NRSV). Such comparisons are not intended by the biblical writers to reduce God to the level of a creature, nor should *we* drag God down to that level by careless thought and speech.

Finally, by instructing us to pray to God as our Father *in heaven*, Jesus is teaching us that God is infinitely beyond our categories of thought and language—for heaven is the realm and reality of God the Creator, not the world of finite creatures such as ourselves. Because God is our Father *in heaven*, God is not *like* our human fathers. This does not mean fathers on earth should not aspire to be more like God! Of course they should, as should everyone. We are all called to grow in the godliness revealed to us through Jesus. To adapt an idea from Johnson, the problem is not that God is called "Father" but that more fathers are not like God.[4]

So "Father" is symbolic language, and especially as our *Abba*, God is symbolized as loving, caring, deeply invested and involved,

---

3. Elizabeth Johnson, *Consider Jesus: Waves of Renewal in Christology* (New York: Crossroad Publishing, 1992), 108.

4. In *Consider Jesus*, Johnson actually uses this wording about Jesus and his maleness (109).

and knowing our needs. In this light, may we be emboldened to approach the throne of grace as God's beloved children who are not averse to praying, "Our Father, who art in heaven."

⚒ 2 ⚒
HALLOWED BE YOUR NAME

Our Father, who art in heaven
Hallowed be your name

The word "hallowed" means, essentially, "holy"—and certainly early Christianity inherited from the Jewish tradition this basic idea that God's name *is* holy, to be treated with utmost respect, worship, and awe. One of the Ten Commandments is, "Thou shalt not take the name of the Lord thy God in vain" (Exodus 20:7, KJV), which is less about cursing and much more about treating God's name lightly, or as some kind of magical incantation that we can control. Because God is *holy*—wholly set apart from all people and things in creation and, indeed, from the entirety of creation itself—God's name is not to be treated like just any old name.

This second line of the Lord's Prayer reminds us that, even as we boldly approach God in prayer as "our Father," we ought always keep in heart and mind that God is not our good-luck charm, not a rabbit's foot, not under our management, and certainly not subject to our puny understanding or agenda. All of this can be terribly easy to say but far more difficult to practice. To enter into God's presence in prayer is to enter, humbly and boldly and tremblingly, into the presence of holiness.

Obviously, though, God does not need *us* to inform God that God is holy. "Hallowed be your name" is not so much a statement of theological fact as it is a prayer, a *yearning* that Jesus teaches us to feel. It is much truer to this prayer to think of it this way: *Our Father, who art in heaven, may we keep your name holy by our very lives, by all we say and do.* We are praying that we will remember God's holy name, God's holy character, and live accordingly. We are praying that our lives will align with, and so proclaim, the holiness of God.

This calling—to be holy in accordance with God's holiness—is the calling that God places upon the people of Israel, but their prophets, especially Ezekiel, bemoan how often the people fall short of this holy calling:

> *I scattered them among the nations,[1] and they were dispersed through the countries; in accordance with their conduct and their deeds I judged them. But when they came to the nations, wherever they came, they profaned my holy name, in that it was said of them, "These are the people of the LORD, and yet they had to go out*

---

1. It is important to remember always that, in Old Testament writings, the word generally translated as "nations" means gentile (i.e., non-Jewish) ethnicities and cultures. Israel's relationships with "the nations" is one of the most enduring themes in the Bible.

of his land." But I had concern for my holy name, which the house of Israel had profaned among the nations to which they came. Therefore say to the house of Israel, Thus says the LORD GOD: It is not for your sake, O house of Israel, that I am about to act, but for the sake of my holy name, which you have profaned among the nations to which you came. I will sanctify my great name, which has been profaned among the nations, and which you have profaned among them; and the nations shall know that I am the LORD, says the LORD GOD, when through you I display my holiness before their eyes.
(Ezekiel 36:19–23, NRSV)

The apostle Paul draws on this Old Testament theme when he writes in his letter to the Romans, "But if you call yourself a Jew and rely on the law and boast of your relation to God . . . will you not teach yourself? You that abhor idols, do you rob temples? You that boast in the law, do you dishonor God by breaking the law? For, as it is written, 'The name of God is blasphemed among the Gentiles because of you'" (Romans 2:17, 21, 22b–24, NRSV). Despite these harsh judgments, Judaism even into the present day demonstrates great concern for sanctification of the name of the Holy One.

As much as we who are Christians can learn from this deeply Jewish commitment to sanctify God's name in all we say and do, we finally believe that God's promise through the prophet Ezekiel—to "display my holiness before their eyes" through the people of Israel—found its fulfillment in Jesus Christ our Lord. It is in Jesus's own person, words, and works that we believe divine holiness has been manifested to us. His life is the perfect hallowing of God's name. Thus, he does not simply teach us to pray that God's name would be sanctified in our lives together as the church, such that God would be glorified among all the various peoples of the world. Jesus also teaches what sort of life accomplishes this lofty goal. "You [plural] are the light of the world. A town built on a hill cannot be hidden. In the same way, let your light shine before others, that they may see your good deeds and glorify your Father in heaven" (Matthew 5:14, 16).

The Sermon on the Mount as a whole offers a compelling portrait of the sort of human living that hallows God's name, and this theme reaches its zenith when Jesus describes the lavish love of God for all people. In Matthew 5:43, Jesus says, "You have heard that it was said, 'Love your neighbor'"—this much coming from the Torah, or the Law of Moses (Leviticus 19:18). But then Jesus adds, "'and hate your enemy.'" Although the people of Israel are never explicitly commanded by God to hate their enemies, there certainly are commands in the Torah about *exterminating* their enemies (Deut. 7:1–6, 20:1–18); further, it would be difficult not to appeal to the famous prayer of David in Psalm 139 (vv. 19, 21–22):

> *If only you, God, would slay the wicked!*
> *Away from me, you who are bloodthirsty!*
>
> *Do I not hate those who hate you, LORD,*
> *and abhor those who are in rebellion against you?*
> *I have nothing but hatred for them;*
> *I count them my enemies.*

Thus, it would not be difficult to assume that hallowing God's name—keeping it holy and above reproach—could require a seething hatred of anyone and anything that might sully or be-

To pray "hallowed be your
name" is to be moved from
our comfortable prejudices into
God's calling to love all people—
including those whom we consider
to be the least lovable.

smirch God's holiness. But we know that Jesus teaches and lives a different hallowing of God's name:

> *But I tell you, love your enemies and pray for those who persecute you, that you may be children of your Father in heaven. He causes his sun to rise on the evil and the good, and sends [the blessing of] rain on the righteous and the unrighteous. If you love those who love you, what reward will you get? Are not even the tax collectors doing that? And if you greet only your own people, what are you doing more than others? Do not even pagans do that? Be perfect, therefore, as your heavenly Father is perfect.*
> *(Matthew 5:44–48)*

The daunting conclusion of this passage—"Be perfect as your heavenly Father is perfect"—is an obvious and intentional echo of Leviticus 19:2, where God calls upon Israel, "Be holy, because I, the LORD your God, am holy." The people of Israel are to sanctify God's holy name by a collective life of obedience to God's laws.[2] The Sermon on the Mount replaces the adjective "holy" with the term "perfect" (*teleios* in the Greek, meaning "complete" or "mature").

---

2. God's holy name is signified in most English translations of the Old Testament by the use of the diminutive-caps LORD. The Hebrew term, transliterated into English, is *YHWH*. Observant Jews do not pronounce this name out of deference for its holiness. Christians generally have not been nearly so circumspect; the older, more traditional English rendering of the name is "Jehovah," while more contemporary usage, particularly in some worship choruses, has been "Yahweh." Jewish practice has been to substitute the term *Adonai*, or "Lord," in place of the divine name. Indeed, many observant Jews simply employ the Hebrew term *Hashem*, "the Name," as a way of referring to God while maintaining the sanctity of the divine name.

It is significant that Jesus teaches that the most faithful way of imitating God's character, or of upholding God's holy name, is by *indiscriminately* loving all people in the same way God does. Jesus contrasts such living with that of tax collectors and gentiles (or "pagans"), who do what comes naturally by loving and welcoming those who are like them, those with whom they are comfortable, those with whom they feel safe and secure. Of course, this behavior is natural for any human. The term "pagans" in this scripture ("gentiles" in NRSV) is meant to demonstrate the contrast of Israel's calling to be a light to all the nations through the sanctification of God's name. The surprising move that Jesus makes, of course, is to teach us that this hallowing of God's name is accomplished through loving our so-called enemies, through welcoming those who are strange or alien to us, through praying for those who persecute us. This kind of love is a far cry from much that passes for Christianity nowadays. To pray "hallowed be your name" is to be moved from our comfortable prejudices into God's calling to love all people—including those whom we consider to be the least lovable.

Jesus not only teaches this way of hallowing God's name, but he also radically practices it. According to the Gospel of Mark, the day after his triumphal entry into Jerusalem, Jesus enters the temple precinct and begins overturning the moneychangers' tables and driving out those selling and buying sacrificial animals. This act occurs in the outer courtyard of the temple—the area designated as a place of prayer for non-Jews. It is the one area of the vast temple grounds where non-Jews are allowed, which is probably why some enterprising Jewish merchants think they should set up convenience stores here; after all, who will really be concerned about a sacred space for gentile prayers?

Jesus, apparently. As he cleanses the temple, Mark reports that he says, "Is it not written: 'My house will be called a house of prayer for all nations'?" (11:17). Remember that "the nations" is the typical biblical designation for non-Jewish peoples or ethnicities. Jesus, in this great prophetic act, is sanctifying God's holy name by reasserting God's love for all people of creation, not simply for Israel. Jesus's act is reminiscent of Ezekiel's prophetic message that God's holy name has been profaned among the nations—among the non-Jewish peoples of the world—by Israel's behavior. Such prophetic words and actions do not go unnoticed, so it should not surprise us that Mark adds, "And when the chief priests and the scribes heard it, they kept looking for a way to kill him" (v. 18, NRSV).

If all of this is a legitimate interpretation of the prayer, "hallowed be your name"—may our lives be such that we sanctify your name, that we bring honor to who you are, O God—then this is a profoundly countercultural, and thus a very dangerous, prayer. Jesus is crucified mere days after he cleanses (or "sanctifies," or "makes holy," or *hallows*) the temple in the Gospel of Mark. May God grant us the grace and courage not simply to mouth the words but also to live such bold lives as this.

⤳ 3 ⤲
YOUR KINGDOM COME

Your kingdom come, your will be done
On earth as it is in heaven

God's Kingdom

Back in the early 1980s, when I was a new and terribly green pastor, I received an odd piece of advice from a retired pastor. "Mike," he said to me, "You stay there with those folks in La Puente for a good long while." (That wasn't the odd part!) Then he added, "You stay there awhile and build your kingdom."

That really is a strange way for one pastor to talk to another. "Build your kingdom." It had never occurred to me to think of the relationship between a pastor and a congregation as something like that between a monarch and their realm! It's just wrong. The only kingdom any Christian—let alone a pastor—should be interested in is God's. This fellow was a good, kind, well-meaning man, but theologically and pastorally, this advice is way off. A pastor is not royalty, and should never act the part. Further, a Christian congregation is not a pastor's realm to rule.

There's another problem with this advice. Even if we were to shift the idea from the pastor as ruler to God as ruler—which is a pretty good idea—it's still biblically incorrect and theologically dangerous to presume that *we* build God's kingdom. We are not builders of God's kingdom. Only God can bring about the kingdom of God. Granted, there is the beautiful fact that God desires to work with us, that God in loving-kindness does call upon us to be co-laborers with God—but we do not take it upon ourselves to "build the kingdom." In the Gospel of Luke Jesus says to his disciples, "Do not be afraid, little flock, for your Father has been pleased to give you the kingdom" (12:32). Isn't that wonderful? God is pleased to give us the kingdom! It's not something we build; it is something we receive as a *gift*.

Unfortunately, it is difficult, especially for American Christians, to shake the notion that we are kingdom builders. This error seems to be the root of much confusion between American Christianity and nationalism. Too often we have mistaken our political nation for God's kingdom. We seem—both on the right and left ends of the political spectrum—to assume that God's kingdom either will or will not be advanced by the people we vote into political office. This assumption is a tragic mistake. God's kingdom is not synonymous with the United States of America, nor is the USA even a special representative *of* God's kingdom. To claim any such thing is heresy. Biblically speaking, the people who represent—not build!—God's kingdom are usually called "the church," and God's church, the body of Christ, transcends all

*When we pray for
God's kingdom to come,
we acknowledge that
none of our kingdoms
is God's.*

national, ethnic, linguistic, cultural, racial, and other boundaries. Yet, through the centuries, many Christians have continued to confuse their particular demographic identities—whether national, ethnic, denominational, or something else—with the reality of God's reign and rule. Praying *"your* kingdom come" should always provide a check on our utopian presumptions that we understand the nature of God's reign, that we share God's perspective on the world, or even that we know what's good for everybody. God's kingdom is God's—not ours.

We recall that even God's own people, Israel, allowed themselves to be taken in by the false hope of nationalism. In the Bible, God clearly desires Israel to be a uniquely set-apart representative people, a divinely called people who embody God's reign and rule in the world. But, as we read in 1 Samuel, Israel's elders gather before the prophet Samuel and say, "You are old, and your sons do not follow your ways; now appoint a king to lead us, such as all the other nations have" (8:5). Samuel tries to warn them by reminding them how kings behave. A king will conscript the young men into military service, will force the remaining young men to work his fields, will force the women into his service, will take the best of what the orchards produce, and will tax everyone to death (vv. 10–18).

Presumably God as King would operate differently! When we pray for God's kingdom to come, we acknowledge that none of our kingdoms is God's. Simply praying this is already a judgment upon our pretensions to erect a kingdom that could possibly represent God's character, will, and intentions. This is why we pray, instead, "Your kingdom come." We learn from Jesus to pray for the coming—the full arrival—of God's reign and rule. If, as we have read from Luke's Gospel, God is pleased to give us the kingdom, then why does Jesus instruct us to ask for it? What is the nature of this kingdom that God gives yet for the coming of which we still must pray?

Matthew 3 tells us that when John the Baptist appears in the wilderness of Judea, his message is simple: "Repent, for the kingdom of heaven has come near" (v. 2). It is certainly no coincidence that in the very next chapter we read that Jesus, after his baptism by John and his time of temptation in the wilderness, begins his public ministry by proclaiming, "Repent, for the kingdom of heaven has come near" (4:17). Matthew uses an identical one-sentence description of the preaching and message from both. *Repent! Turn around! Turn from your life of sin and turn toward God, because God's kingdom is drawing near!*

Even though John and Jesus apparently preach a similar message, we should recall that, a little later, John sends a question to Jesus from his prison cell, via a couple of his followers: "Are you the one who is to come, or should we expect someone else?" (11:3). John the Baptist, of all people, asks that question, which suggests that *his* ideas about the coming of God's kingdom do not correspond particularly well with Jesus's actions. Why not? What is *John* expecting, we might wonder. And what should *we* be expecting, when we pray, "Your kingdom come"?

This much is certain: if we truly do pray for the coming of God's kingdom, God's righteous rule on earth, then that reorders all the other cares, concerns, and agendas of our lives. A little later in the Sermon on the Mount, after teaching his disciples the prayer we are exploring, Jesus assures them (and us!) that God will care for all of our needs: "So do not worry, saying, 'What shall we eat?'

or 'What shall we drink?' or 'What shall we wear?' For the pagans [the worldly folks] run after all these things, and your heavenly Father knows that you need them. But seek first his kingdom and his righteousness [or justice], and all these things will be given to you as well" (6:31–33). So we pray for the coming of God's kingdom, we receive the kingdom as God's good pleasure to give, we expect God's kingdom, and we turn from our sins and even our legitimate concerns for our daily needs, all to allow God's kingdom to become our one true obsession! *Your kingdom come.*

Not long after, in Matthew 10, Jesus sends out his disciples on a trial missionary run, instructing them, "Do not go among the Gentiles or enter any town of the Samaritans. Go rather to the lost sheep of Israel. As you go, proclaim this message: 'The kingdom of heaven has come near'" (vv. 5b–7). Then Jesus adds, "Heal the sick, raise the dead, cleanse those who have leprosy, drive out demons" (v. 8a). These are signs of the coming of God's kingdom: people being made well, hearts and lives and bodies restored, creation being renewed by its Creator. That is good news! Jesus constantly assures us that God knows our needs and tends to our needs.

Jesus, in fact, is the presence of the kingdom and the guarantee that God freely grants us the kingdom, which is none other than God's righteous, just, and life-giving rule. When some of his enemies accuse him of casting out demons by the power of the prince of demons, Jesus rejects this first of all as an example of terrible logic. Then he adds, "But if it is by the Spirit of God that I drive out demons, then the kingdom of God has come upon you" (12:28). How has the kingdom of God come to us? In the very person of Jesus the Messiah, the anointed one of God, who is filled and guided by the Holy Spirit of God. Wherever Jesus is, there the kingdom is already showing up.

But if that is so, then why *does* John the Baptist have second thoughts about Jesus? Why would he want to know if Jesus is the one they've been waiting for or if they should keep waiting for someone else? What a sad, even tragic, question this is! I'm not blaming or belittling John the Baptist; I'm just trying to get my head and heart around the sense of confusion, and even disappointment, that must inspire his question. It can only mean that John has very different ideas about the coming of the Messiah and God's kingdom.

It is likely that John would be just as shocked as Jesus's disciples by what we read in Matthew 18: "At that time the disciples came to Jesus and asked, 'Who, then, is the greatest in the kingdom of heaven?'" (v. 1). By the way, isn't it interesting that Jesus doesn't say, "Well, duh! Obviously I am!" Nor does he, in this instance, say that John the Baptist is right up there at the top (see Matthew 11:11). Instead, to answer their self-serving question, "He called a little child to him, and placed the child among them. And he said, 'Truly I tell you, unless you change and become like little children, you will never enter the kingdom of heaven. Therefore, whoever takes the lowly position of this child is the greatest in the kingdom of heaven. And whoever welcomes one such child in my name welcomes me'" (18:2–5). Seriously, what kind of kingdom is this, Jesus? Little bothersome children with their snotty noses? Whoever welcomes one such child in Jesus's name actually is welcoming Jesus? Where is the glory in that? Where is the power? Where is the world-shattering *might*? Where is the ax

45

How often have you and
I prayed for the coming of
God's kingdom and then
entirely overlooked it
right before our eyes?

laid to the tree trunk? I think those might be the sort of questions rolling around in John's heart and mind in his prison cell.

Of course, we remember what happens in the very next chapter, Matthew 19: "Then people brought little children to Jesus for him to place his hands on them and pray for them. But the disciples rebuked them. Jesus said, 'Let the little children come to me, and do not hinder them, for the kingdom of heaven belongs to such as these'" (vv. 13–14). Why? Most scholars believe it has nothing to do with any inherently special quality of childhood but rather because, in the social pecking order of Jesus's culture, children count for very little. They are unimportant; they are nobodies. They are overlooked and undervalued. *To them belongs the kingdom of God.*

So we ask once more, what are we praying for when we pray for the coming of God's kingdom? After all, in one important sense, God's kingdom has already come in Jesus: in all he said and did and taught, in his deeds of healing, in his humility all the way to the cross, he embodied God's kingdom. He was crucified by this sinful world for that very reason. But the world cannot destroy God's kingdom. And God is pleased to give to Jesus's "little flock" this very kingdom of righteousness and peace, of justice and love. It is also, surprisingly enough, a kingdom of humility. "For I am gentle and humble in heart," Jesus says to us (Matthew 11:29), and he also came to earth in the humble station of a little child.

So may we look for the coming of God's kingdom. It comes in the humility of the unnoticed, the dismissed, the unimportant, undervalued, and the marginalized. How often have you and I prayed for the coming of God's kingdom and then entirely overlooked it right before our eyes? Look for the kingdom in unexpected places and people. And when you see even one such person, receive, welcome, and embrace them in Jesus's name. Jesus assures us that we'll be receiving him when we do.

God's Will

It is highly likely that our praying that God's will be done on earth is essentially the same as praying that God's kingdom might come. It is a typical way of emphasizing a point in Jewish writing to say the same thing in two different ways. Think, for instance, of "Search me, God, and know my heart; test me and know my anxious thoughts" (Psalm 139:23), or "Shout it aloud, do not hold back. Raise your voice like a trumpet" (Isaiah 58:1). So what might this meditation add that is new and different from the previous one? How is praying for God's will to be done different from praying that God's kingdom might come?

One point that stands out prominently is that, with this prayer, we encounter not only Jesus's teaching but also, later, Jesus's own compelling embodiment of this very prayer. We remember that the Synoptic Gospels all describe Jesus's deep and mighty struggling in prayer in the garden of Gethsemane, just prior to his arrest. Mark, for example, tells us that Jesus, already "distressed and troubled" (14:33), says to his inner circle of Peter, James, and John, "My soul is overwhelmed with sorrow to the point of death. Stay here and keep watch" (v. 34). Then he throws himself down to the ground and prays, "*Abba*, Father, everything is possible for you. Take this cup from me" (v. 36). But Jesus doesn't stop there. He continues his prayer by affirming the will of God: "Yet not what I will, but what you will" (v. 36). Jesus's prayer is that God's will be accomplished in his own life as it is in heaven—which, presumably, means *perfectly*, or completely.

Let us not sweep Jesus's own struggle under the grass of Gethsemane. Luke graphically reports that, "being in anguish, he prayed more earnestly, and his sweat was like drops of blood falling to the ground" (22:44). His struggle is real. The description of Jesus in Gethsemane is one of the biblical passages that early church theologians relied on to demonstrate that Jesus exercises true volition—that he experiences the hardships of real temptation and excruciatingly difficult choices.[1] He has not merely glided through life, and his prayers in Gethsemane are not a puppet show. Jesus experiences the intensity of his own will, expressed in the fundamental human instinct of survival. But in these incredibly trying moments in Gethsemane, he himself prays the same way he has taught us to pray: *your will be done.*

The book of Hebrews uses similar passionate language to describe Jesus in prayer: "During the days of Jesus's life on earth, he offered up prayers and petitions with fervent cries and tears to the one who could save him from death, and he was heard because of his reverent submission" (5:7). Perhaps the most remarkable observation about Jesus in this passage is that *he has been heard.* That is what matters. No, Jesus is not spared the suffering that awaits him in his passion and crucifixion. But through it all, *he is heard.* That is all he needs, and finally it is all *we* need: to be *heard* by the One who listens to every prayer, every yearning, every tear and lament. Jesus is heard.

---

1. See Lodahl and Cordero, *Renewal in Love*, 86–92.

Hebrews, in fact, goes on to say that, even as God's Son, Jesus "learned obedience from what he suffered and, once made perfect [through his sufferings, struggles, and trials], he became the source of eternal salvation for all who obey him" (5:8–9). Having learned what it means to obey through the struggles and temptations of life, Jesus now stands as the one to whom we are to render our obedience. Obedience is not automatic; it is not the work of robots. It demands the offering up of our wills to God—but it never eliminates or destroys our will. God does not and will not erase or negate the power of agency that God has entrusted to us. This, perhaps, is why the wise Jewish philosopher Martin Buber wrote in his classic work, *I and Thou*, "'Let your will be done' is all [we pray], but truth goes on to say for [us]: 'through me whom you need.'"[2]

Does God actually *need* us? Generally, Christian theology has answered that question in the negative. God is the omnipotent Creator and Sustainer of all things and thus, in Paul's words to the Athenians, "does not live in shrines made by human hands, nor is he served by human hands, as though he needed anything, since he himself gives to all mortals life and breath and all things" (Acts 17:24–25, NRSV). A God who *needs* does not sound like much of a God at all. But this acknowledgment only raises a further question: could God *choose* to need creatures like us?

Think about the creation story in Genesis 1. Here we read that God "created humankind in his image, in the image of God he created them; male and female he created them" (v. 27, NRSV).

2. Martin Buber, *I and Thou*, trans. Walter Kaufmann (New York: Touchstone, 1971), 131.

*The world cannot
destroy God's kingdom.*

God creates humanity then immediately entrusts humanity with the task of having "dominion . . . over every living thing that moves upon the earth" (v. 28, NRSV). One might wonder why. Why doesn't God simply exercise dominion? Why entrust such a momentous task to mere creatures as we? What is the Creator trying to accomplish by calling human beings to be God's representatives?

Or think about God calling on Moses to become Israel's liberator. From a burning bush God says to Moses, "I have indeed seen the misery of my people in Egypt. I have heard them crying out because of their slave drivers, and I am concerned about their suffering. So I have come down to rescue them from the hand of the Egyptians" (Exodus 3:7–8a). It is not difficult to imagine Moses thinking this is a great thing that God will do, and to offer applause and praise for such a mighty God.

But what does he think when God adds, "So now, go. I am sending you to Pharaoh to bring my people the Israelites out of Egypt" (v. 10)? Actually, it is no mystery: Moses spends the next two chapters' worth of dialogue trying to convince God how bad an idea this is. God persists. But why? Why does God need Moses for this task? Why would God need *anyone* for this task?

Moses flat-out refuses: "Pardon your servant, Lord. Please send someone else" (4:13). Significantly, Exodus narrates that "then the LORD's anger burned against Moses" (4:14). This is a perfect opportunity for God to reply, "Fine! I'll do it myself!" and then perhaps snuff out Moses's puny existence with a blast from the burning bush.

Instead, this God whose anger burns against Moses finds a compromise: "What about your brother, Aaron the Levite? I know he can speak well. He is already on his way to meet you, and he will be glad to see you. You shall speak to him and put words in his mouth; I will help both of you speak and will teach you what to do" (4:14–15). Strangely, this omnipotent God insists on working with, rather than in spite of, or over the heads of, such finite and fragile humans as Moses and Aaron. There is a mystery here, and it is the mystery of divine love that seeks to include, to entrust, to collaborate with us creatures of dust, so feeble and frail.

So perhaps Buber, well and deeply schooled in such stories of the Hebrew Bible, was not so far wrong to suggest that we pray, "Your will be done—through us, whom you need." If this is so, then perhaps God, in infinite love, desires our true and willing cooperation in accomplishing the divine will. God, we must suppose, is not interested in forcing God's way, or in unilaterally shoving us into kingdom life. God, revealed in Jesus is, "gentle and humble in heart" (Matthew 11:29), and thus invites us to faithful discipleship but will not coerce us into it. "May your will be done on earth," in our earthly lives, as it is in heaven—and grant us the grace and strength to choose so to live.

But just because God does not force us to do the divine will does not mean there are no consequences either way. Near the end of the Sermon on the Mount, Jesus warns, "Not everyone who says to me, 'Lord, Lord,' will enter the kingdom of heaven, but only the one who does the will of my Father who is in heaven" (Matthew 7:21). We may pray, "your will be done," but Jesus insists that *we* are actually to do God's will. Further, given that Jesus's warning comes virtually at the end of the sermon, it is safe to assume that the Sermon on the Mount is an essential summary of what exactly God wills. In Luke's version, Jesus asks pointedly, "Why do you call me, 'Lord, Lord,' and do not do what I say?"

(Luke 6:46). What Jesus teaches us is how God wills for us to live. But God cannot and will not do that for us, or in our place.

The fact that Jesus teaches us to pray that God's will might be done on earth—in our very lives—as it is in heaven already indicates that God's will was not in Jesus's day, nor is it in our time, actually being accomplished. This is an important insight for those who might assume that, because God is God, whatever happens in the world must ultimately be what God wants to happen. This is obviously not the case. If God wills that there be no murder, adultery, coveting, or bearing false witness—just to draw upon a few of the Ten Commandments—then obviously God's will is constantly being ignored and, thus, frustrated. More radically, if God's will is that no man look upon a woman with lust (Matthew 5:28), or that no one become angry with a brother or sister, or call someone else a fool (5:22), or that we all love our enemies (5:44), it seems patently obvious that, on a regular and virtually universal basis, God's will is very far from being done.

God's will is what God desires to see in our lives and in the world as a whole. In two separate conflicts with Pharisees, Jesus quotes divine speech from Hosea 6:6, "I desire mercy, not sacrifice" (Matthew 9:13; 12:7). Jesus quotes this prophetic text to defend his disciples' plucking of grain on the Sabbath because they are hungry, and also to defend his own table fellowship with "many tax collectors and sinners" (9:10). For Jesus, God's desire—God's will—is not so much worship or sacrifice offered to God but mercy or compassion extended toward all people. In Matthew's Gospel especially, Jesus insists that God *desires* mercy, but the fact that Jesus is quoting this to people who, as far as Jesus is concerned, do not exemplify mercy but instead hard-hearted superiority already means that what

God *desires* is not what God is *getting*. Jesus demonstrates God's mercy toward tax-collecting traitors and other assorted sinners, but apparently he is in rare company. God desires mercy and not sacrifice, but mostly God is getting ritual sacrifices (think of what we now call "worship" in Sunday services) rather than mercy toward those who most need it.

We might wonder whether—when we pray, "your will be done on earth as it is in heaven"—we are asking God simply to usher in a whole new world where God's will cannot be frustrated, where what God desires simply *is* accomplished in our lives, where human obedience (or lack thereof) has become a non-issue. In the late eighteenth century, John Wesley raised this question in his fascinating sermon "The General Spread of the Gospel." His initial reply to the question seems to leave no doubt: "Only suppose the Almighty to act *irresistibly*, and the thing is done; yea, with just the same ease as when God said, 'Let there be light' and there was light."[3] The omnipotent Creator of all things surely could bring about a world in which God's will is done as it is in heaven.

But why hasn't God done so? What is God waiting for? Why has God not acted "irresistibly," in such a way that no creature could possibly resist what God wants? Wesley answers his own question for us: "But then man would be man no longer; his inmost nature would be changed. He would no longer be a moral agent, any more than the sun or the wind . . . [he] would no longer be capable of virtue or vice, of reward or punishment."[4] Wesley believed that human agency and responsibility are values to God

---

3. John Wesley, "The General Spread of the Gospel," *The Works of John Wesley* (Nashville: Abingdon Press, 1984), 6:280.
4. Wesley, "The General Spread of the Gospel."

so important, so great, that God has no interest in overriding or negating them. In other words, this is not about God's inability but about God's character. God—in infinite, matchless, everlasting love—longs to labor *with* us frail creatures rather than *in spite of* us, or over our heads. If Wesley was right about this, then we may find ourselves once again edging toward Buber's striking addition to the prayer, "Let your will be done . . . through us whom you need."

Within hours of praying that God's will be done, Jesus was gasping desperately for air as he bled on a Roman cross. Are you and I really willing to pray this prayer? May it never be simply cheap, memorized words. By the marvelous grace of God, may the will of our loving God be accomplished in our everyday lives and in all the everyday situations and relationships in which we find ourselves. *Your kingdom come, your will be done on earth as it is in heaven.*

❧ 4 ❧
GIVE US THIS DAY

Give us this day our daily bread

In this simple petition, we are reminded that we are needy creatures—as if we need a reminder! In fact, we often seem intent on suppressing this reality, but no amount of denial or rationalization can erase the simple truth that we need to eat. We have mouths and teeth with which to ingest and chew and stomachs that like to be filled. And the "we" is everyone; indeed, it is every creature on God's good green earth. (Maybe they don't all have teeth and stomachs, but the point remains!) The fact that we must eat is a strong indication that we are not self-sufficient, self-reliant, isolated beings. We exist together in a vast, complex living system of creatures that both require and provide nourishment. This is our creaturely state. One of the recurring biblical descriptions of this reality is "flesh." The prophet Isaiah compares the flesh of humanity to grass because it is temporary, transitory, fragile (see Isaiah 40:6).

Correspondingly, Scripture repeatedly proclaims that God, the Creator of all flesh, is therefore also the ultimate Provider for all flesh, or all creatures. In the words of the beautifully stunning 104th Psalm:

> *O LORD, how diverse are your works! In wisdom you have made them all; the earth is full of your creatures.*
>
> *All of them look to you to give them their food when they feel hunger; when you give to them, they gather and gobble it up; when you open your hand, they are satisfied with good things.*
> *(Psalm 104:24, 27–28, author's translation)*

This biblical teaching that God is the source of our nourishing food is the reason it is always good, right, and proper to give thanks to God before we eat a meal. The rabbis taught that what distinguishes human beings from all other creatures is that we can, and should, offer thanks to God before we eat. But even on this point, Scripture hints otherwise; Psalm 104 not only proclaims that all creatures look to God for their nourishment but also more specifically insists that "the lions roar for their prey and seek their food from God" (v. 21). Commenting on this text, John Wesley suggested that a lion's roar is "a kind of natural prayer to God."[1] The point is not that lions are conscious of God, although Wesley might have suggested that, to the extent that such crea-

---

1. Wesley, *Explanatory Notes upon the Old Testament* (Salem, OH: Schmul, 1975).

tures' capacities allow, they have their own sense for God and seek their food from their ultimate Provider. If nothing else, such biblical lines underscore the radical neediness of all creatures to find food, to be fed, and to sustain their lives through the consumption of other life. Jesus assures us that our heavenly Father feeds the birds of the air—sometimes with seed, sometimes with fruit, sometimes with worms, but always with the material energies of God's own good creation. Humans participate in this same cycle.

Another psalm assures us that God knows our frame— knows how we are put together and what it takes to keep us going. Our Maker "knows how we are formed, he remembers that we are dust" (103:14). The term "dust," like "flesh" and "grass," signifies once more our frail and fragile bearing in the world. As one of my most beloved seminary professors, Rob Staples, liked to remind his students, "We are all only one heartbeat from the ground we walk on." Indeed, the Hebrew word for "human" is *adam*, which comes directly from *adamah*, which means "dirt" or "ground."[2] Remember the Creator's words to our ancestors, "By the sweat of your brow you will eat your food until you return to the ground, since from it you were taken; for dust you are and to dust you will return" (Genesis 3:19). In the Old Testament especially, dust is, not surprisingly, the stuff beneath our feet but also what gets carried in the winds. The biblical imagery of dust carries the implication of dirt that is easily scattered and blown away, here today, over there tomorrow, finite and frail and mortal. And

---

2. The English word "human" itself is derived from the Latin designation for dirt or ground, *humus.*

*God works in and
through the daily grind
of creaturely existence to
bring nourishment to us
humble creatures.*

thus we truly do need "our daily bread" to sustain our fragile lives, to keep our bodies from premature disintegration.

The language "our daily bread" surely brings to mind the story of the people Israel in their wilderness wanderings, sustained by God's gift of the daily bread called manna (which, according to Exodus 16:15, essentially means, "What is this stuff?"). God instructs them to gather just enough for each day, except for on Fridays, during which they are to gather enough for that day and the following day, the Sabbath, as well. Perhaps for this reason some ancient versions of the Lord's Prayer read, "give us today our bread for tomorrow" or "the bread *of* tomorrow;" this version of the prayer connects the Jewish observance of the Sabbath with the anticipation of the age to come—the end of the world as we know it. In this context, the Jewish experience of Sabbath is understood to be a foretaste of the world to come, a slice of eternity making its beautiful presence felt at the culmination of each week.[3] The bread for tomorrow would likely signify, in this case, the bread of the messianic banquet (see Matthew 8:11, 26:29). In turn, this interpretation coincides nicely with, "Your kingdom come, your will be done on earth as it is in heaven." In this wording and interpretation, the prayer both reflects and encourages our yearning for God's eternal Sabbath to enter fully into creation—the great day of the Lord during which we shall eat the bread of tomorrow.

But let us return to the more mundane reading of this prayer. "Give us this day our daily bread" reinforces not only the conviction that God is our Provider but also that God works in and

---

3. For the classic and exceedingly moving treatment of this idea and practice in Jewish tradition, see Abraham Joshua Heschel, *The Sabbath: Its Meaning for Modern Man* (New York: Farrar, Strauss and Giroux, 2005).

through the daily grind of creaturely existence to bring nourishment to us humble creatures. God spoke through the prophet Hosea, "I led them with cords of human kindness, with ties of love. To them I was like one who lifts a little child to the cheek, and I bent down to feed them" (11:4). It is true that the Israelites grow tired of eating the same old thing, and it is not hard to imagine ourselves airing the same gripe. Variety is the spice of life! But Jesus instructs us toward humbler expectations: let us simply ask God for the bread we knead for today.

If God is willing to feed the wandering Israelites, and if Jesus encourages us to pray for our daily bread, we might justifiably ask if there are any people whom God has no interest in feeding. It is a sobering question. More than twenty thousand people die every day from hunger or hunger-related causes. This means that roughly every four seconds—perhaps about the time it takes to read this sentence—another person will have starved to death. This situation is the most dire in sub-Saharan Africa, followed by Asia, then Latin America—the peoples whose ancestors endured Western European and North American colonization. The effects of this tragic history continue into this very moment, and even wealthy countries have their own hungry people. Nevertheless, North Americans and Western Europeans consume an unjust ratio of the world's nutritional goods. Collectively, we are consuming far more than our share while too many others are starving to death. Is this what our heavenly Father desires?

When we pray, "Give us this day our daily bread," who is "us?" It obviously is, first, Christian believers, Jesus's followers around the world. But shall we draw the line there? Shall we not extend our sense of who is included in "us?" If we are not among those who hunger, do we simply pat ourselves on the back for being blessed and move on?

Since Jesus is the full embodiment of God's kingdom on earth, we are wise to consult the Gospel testimony about Jesus in regard to this question. The only miracle during Jesus's earthly ministry that all four Gospels describe is his feeding of the multitudes. In Matthew's account, we read that Jesus sees "a large crowd" (14:14) that has "followed him on foot from the towns" out into "a solitary place," (14:13), and Matthew also tells us that Jesus "had compassion on them and healed their sick" (v. 14). As the day draws to a close, his disciples suggest that Jesus should "send the crowds away, so they can go to the villages and buy themselves some food" (v. 15).

Jesus's reply is striking: "They do not need to go away. You give them something to eat" (v. 16). Notice that there is no checking ID, no lines drawn between worthy and unworthy. Jesus—God incarnate—chooses to feed all the people and to do so through the agency of his disciples. "Taking the five loaves and the two fish and looking up to heaven, he gave thanks and broke the loaves. Then he gave them to the disciples, and the disciples gave them to the people" (v. 19).

This crowd, of course, includes thousands of women and children, who would not typically be on the receiving end of men's table service. Here the bounty of God is shared richly and freely among *all* the people, even those considered lower on the culture's social scale, and without regard for personal spirituality or depth of religious commitment. The simple fact is that everybody is hungry, and God in Christ, through the (probably bewildered) obedience of his disciples, feeds everyone: "they all ate and were satisfied" (v. 20). There can be no doubt that this is a miniature portrait of what God desires for all people, everywhere, at all times.

Thus, when we who call ourselves Jesus's disciples pray, "Give us this day our daily bread," we are constrained by Jesus himself to pray this for all people everywhere, and also to seek actively the venues available to us to become the means whereby God answers our prayer. This is the message to Israel: "For the LORD your God is God of gods and Lord of lords, the great God, mighty and awesome, who shows no partiality and accepts no bribes. He defends the cause of the fatherless and the widow, and loves the foreigner residing among you, giving them food and clothing. And you are to love those who are foreigners, for you yourselves were foreigners in Egypt" (Deuteronomy 10:17–19). Surely the message to the church today is no different and no less. If God demonstrates love toward strangers or foreigners by providing them food and clothing and also calls upon the people of God to love the stranger or the foreigner, is not the implication clear? We love anyone who is strange or different from us as God loves strangers: by giving them food and clothing. One might even suspect that it is precisely in this way that God provides the strangers, the marginalized, the excluded and unwelcome peoples with food and clothing. God cares for the forgotten ones, the excluded ones, the dehumanized ones *through* the caring, and sometimes daring, deeds of God's people.

It finally comes to this: we who have become God's children through Jesus Christ are called upon by God to become like God. Our God desires to feed the hungry. "Give thanks to the LORD, for he is good. His love endures forever. He gives food to every creature. His love endures forever" (Psalm 136:1, 25). Remember that "every creature" means all creatures everywhere—not just humans (Genesis 9:8–17). God "gives to the animals their food, and to the young ravens when they cry" (Psalm 147:9, NRSV).

So when we pray, "Give us this day our daily bread," may we endeavor to make our "us" as expansive as our Creator does, for as John Wesley dearly loved to quote, "The LORD is good to all; he has compassion on all [creatures] he has made" (Psalm 145:9). May it be so! And may we help to make it so.

⤧ 5 ⤦
FORGIVE US

———◆◆◆———

And forgive us our trespasses
As we forgive those who trespass against us

———◆◆◆———

We have come to that part of the Lord's Prayer in which we regularly acknowledge our "trespasses"—which is to say, our sins, our
shortcomings, our stupidities, our lapses in judgment, our frailties, and our failures. There is a lot to confess when we confess our
trespasses!

And we pray it together. Like everything else in the prayer
Jesus teaches, we pray this together, side by side. We acknowledge
before God and before one another that we have said and done
things, and have left other things unsaid and undone, that have
brought harm to other people, to ourselves, and indeed to God's
good creation. We confess together.

In an earlier chapter I briefly mentioned that this is the line
in the prayer that makes people in Holiness denominations a little

nervous. Holiness denominations are strong and vocal champions of sanctification—or, living lives in the power of the Holy Spirit such that the life of sin has been left behind. The tension with this line from the Lord's Prayer, for Holiness Christians, is that people who have been sanctified need not—perhaps even *should* not—pray a prayer that suggests we have sins that need attention.

Allow me to illustrate this by my own experience growing up in a Holiness church. Our pastor during my adolescent years was a wonderful shepherd of people and had a fairly refined sense for liturgy, at least by denominational standards. (I was not particularly aware of this at the time.) For example, we practiced congregational responsive readings of Scripture from the hymnal every Sunday morning. After the pastoral prayer every Sunday, the choir sang the same beautiful response:

Hear our prayer, O Lord;
Hear our prayer, O Lord.
Incline thine ear to us,
And grant us thy peace.

At the end of every Sunday morning service, without exception, we stood and sang the Doxology ("Praise God from Whom All Blessings Flow") as our pastor walked down the middle aisle and out the church doorway, where he stood to greet people as they departed. Perhaps all of this was more common half a century ago, but the point is that, for a Protestant evangelical congregation, there was a fair amount of liturgical predictability and church decorum. This church in which I grew up in the Christian faith was not particularly afraid of ritual. Surely, then, our pastor would not have avoided the Lord's Prayer because he felt it was too formal.

Yet not once do I recall ever praying the Lord's Prayer together in a service during my decade of attendance. Our understanding of holiness was such that it wasn't proper to expect saints to say these words out loud in public. We had an altar where people were invited to confess their sins and seek God's forgiveness, or God's sanctifying grace, but that was different; the whole idea was that *those people* at the altar must have things to confess, while the entirely sanctified really didn't. *(Forgive us our trespasses, indeed!)*

When I was a young pastor, fresh out of seminary and still wet behind the ears, one Sunday morning during the brief interval between Sunday school and morning worship, a congregant knocked on my office door. I opened it and welcomed her in. She wasted no time. "Pastor, I was just in Sunday school, where Audrey* was our substitute teacher. She just told us in class that she has not sinned in fourteen years."

Audrey was a highly visible, upstanding layperson in this congregation. She was the organist, a longtime member of the church, served on the church board, was a conspicuous leader in social events, and knew her Bible. But Audrey also had a biting tongue. She could say things that were hurtful while maintaining a veneer of holiness that smacked of *holier-than-thou*. She could cut people pretty effectively while maintaining a smile that betrayed her aggression, nearly hidden yet visible in a certain glint of her eye. Nobody wanted to cross Audrey. There was a kind of righteous rage always roiling just beneath the surface. We all

---

*Name has been changed.

*To trespass means to say or
do something that crosses a line
into someone else's sensitive space,
even if it is unintentional.*

knew her husband suffered under her oppressive aggression. (They both passed away long ago.) She hadn't sinned in fourteen years?

All I could muster up as a reply, with the hint of a grin, was, "We both know that's not true."

This is the recurring danger in a religious tradition that so emphasizes holiness that it makes little room for confession and repentance. Audrey experienced what she identified as entire sanctification at some point (apparently fourteen years earlier) and, thus, was under the impression that no sins had besmirched her life since—even as she left a goodly number of victims in the wake of her wounding words. Exorbitant claims to holiness lead to rationalization of our own attitudes and behaviors, such that we must be always right. If there's a problem, we project it onto others; it's their fault, not ours. An earlier theologian in our tradition claimed not to have committed a sin in thirty-nine years, beating Audrey's record considerably! But of course, even if this were true at some level, one would suspect that there is something profoundly problematic (if, indeed, not sinful itself) about keeping track like this.

Christians in the Holiness tradition, unfortunately, have often maintained a generous view of ourselves while turning a scrutinizing eye upon others. Further, the notion of having not committed a sin in x years ignores the fact that so much of our mental life—motives, desires, drives, fears—exists on a subconscious level. No wonder David prays, "Search me, God, and know my heart; test me and know my anxious thoughts" (Psalm 139:23). Surely this is the sort of prayer we should all be praying for as long as we live! There is simply too much about ourselves that we do not know or acknowledge.

In *A Plain Account of Christian Perfection,* John Wesley wrote that, for fully devoted Christians, "God is the first object of our love," and that our second responsibility "is to bear the defects of others."[1] This would be the perfect place to add, "and third, to remember always that those others must bear my own defects." Either Wesley overlooked this glaring point—and there is no doubt many others found his own obsessiveness and control issues a lot to deal with!—or else he was slyly smiling as he penned these words, leaving the obvious unsaid. If I think that I, in all my blessed spirituality, have to bear with the defects of other folk while I impose no hardships on others through my words, deeds, or attitudes, I am blind to a basic fact of human interactions. So how do we pray, "forgive us our trespasses," while maintaining a high standard of holy living? Several considerations suggest themselves.

First, let us remember a point from an earlier chapter: this is a social prayer, recited in first-person plural. *"Our* Father . . . forgive us *our* trespasses." Jesus teaches his entire community of disciples to pray this; thus, we can assume that he expects trespasses to occur. People rub other people the wrong way. Some people step on other people's toes. Sometimes people say or do things that hurt others without meaning to or even realizing harm has occurred. These are inevitabilities when any group of people spends any amount of meaningful time with one another in the journey of life. Feelings get hurt. Words wound. Patience gets tested. To trespass means to say or do something that crosses a line into someone else's sensitive space, even if it is unintention-

---

1. Wesley, *A Plain Account of Christian Perfection*, edited and annotated by Randy L. Maddox and Paul W. Chilcote (Kansas City, MO: Beacon Hill Press of Kansas City, 2015), 149.

al or we are convinced that the person who feels wronged is too touchy. In any meaningful community, including (and sometimes especially!) churches, *trespasses inevitably occur.* We are praying together as a people that God would forgive our trespasses, collectively considered.

Further, because this is a corporate prayer, we are acknowledging together that *we* have transgressed others, both inside our community and out. For far too long, American Christians have allowed our faith to be understood and practiced in an individualistic manner. Even if I am confident that I have not committed a sin in the past week, let alone fourteen years, I pray this prayer with my brothers and sisters together because there is no question that, as a people, transgressions have occurred in our midst, by representatives of Christ. We pray together this prayer of confession. In this prayer Jesus is not encouraging his followers to keep a private record of their personal sinlessness. Rather, he urges us to recognize that we are members of a body in which harm has been done by word, deed, and attitude—or by the omission of a word or deed when it was needed.

Once we acknowledge deeply that each of us is but a member of this community of faith and practice called the church—a body with its own foibles and frailties, hurt and hurtfulness, sins and transgressions—then we are in a position also to feel our connections with other Christian believers who lived long before us. We are members of a community that stretches through the annals of two millennia, and it does not take long to recognize the many ways this community has failed to embody God's desires for creation and for every person. The sins of slavery, sexism, anti-Semitism, apartheid, nationalism, violence, child abuse, rampant consumption of resources, just to get the list started—we acknowledge that the church has been and continues to be complicit in these sins. Individual members of the church who do not feel convicted or guilty about this history of transgression have not understood the meaning of the body of Christ. We are in this together, now and throughout history.

We must also note the critical importance Jesus places here on forgiveness of others; we pray for God's forgiveness *even as* we extend that forgiveness to others. Indeed, in the Gospel of Matthew this is the only line of the Lord's Prayer that receives further attention. Jesus immediately elaborates after concluding the prayer, "For if you forgive other people when they sin against you, your heavenly Father will also forgive you. But if you do not forgive others their sins, your Father will not forgive your sins" (6:14–15). Indeed, in Matthew's Gospel, Jesus returns to this critical theme later with the parable of the servant who is forgiven a massive debt by the king but in turn violently imprisons a fellow servant who owes him a pittance. "Shouldn't you have had mercy on your fellow servant just as I had on you?" asks the king (18:33). "In anger his master handed him over to the jailers to be tortured, until he should pay back all he owed. This is how my heavenly Father will treat each of you unless you forgive your brother or sister from your heart" (vv. 34–35). The church is to be a community of forgiveness, rooted deeply in the forgiving love of God that is revealed in Jesus.

Forgiveness can of course be a difficult subject, especially for those who have been deeply wronged or injured by others. We should not speak glibly of forgiveness. Happily, Jesus does not either. Just prior to the parable of the unforgiving servant, Jesus

*True forgiveness includes,
and requires, repentance
and reconciliation.*

teaches his community about the hard work of forgiveness and reconciliation. "If another member of the church sins against you, go and point out the fault when the two of you are alone" (Matthew 18:15a, NRSV). In this way, one avoids publicly shaming the offender, which is a consideration that is important everywhere but particularly in Middle Eastern cultures. Power dynamics can make one-on-one confrontations like this difficult, if not at times impossible. Generally, however, Jesus's teaching is that the hard work of forgiveness and reconciliation includes a frank naming of the transgression by the one who has been harmed. This is not cheap, quick, easy, or glib forgiveness.

Further, Jesus acknowledges that this initial step may not work. "But if you are not listened to, take one or two others along with you, so that every word may be confirmed by the evidence of two or three witnesses" (18:16, NRSV). This instruction hearkens back to the laws of Moses regarding the conviction of someone of "any crime or wrongdoing in connection with any offense that may be committed" (Deuteronomy 19:15, NRSV). In other words, once the accusation of harm goes public, there must be further corroboration "on the evidence of two or three witnesses" (v. 15, NRSV). Once again, we find that forgiveness is not cheap or automatic; there must be admission of guilt by the transgressor if the collective power of multiple witnesses is sufficient to convince or convict the transgressor.

Finally, Jesus's instructions extend beyond this scenario if the one accused of doing harm refuses to acknowledge the action or its destructive nature: "If they still refuse to listen, tell it to the church; and if they refuse to listen even to the church, treat them as you would a pagan or a tax collector" (Matthew 18:17).

The critical point here is that, although Jesus is talking about the necessity of forgiveness, he does not want forgiveness that turns a blind eye to harm, let alone a forgiveness that pretends like nothing happened. True forgiveness includes, and requires, repentance and reconciliation, for the health not simply of individuals but of the entire community.

This is hard, painstaking work! Undoubtedly, this is also why Jesus promises that, "where two or three gather in my name"—recall the two or three witnesses required to name wrongdoing—"there am I with them" (18:20). We often use this promise as a guarantee of Jesus's presence during corporate worship or Bible studies, and this is not wrong to do, but the initial meaning of the text is that Jesus is with his community through the demanding labor of confrontation, forgiveness, and reconciliation ("loosing" in v. 18)—or, contrarily, the heartbreak of denial, refusal, and the festering of the wounds inflicted ("binding" in v. 18).

We cannot ignore the necessity of forgiveness in the midst of Jesus's community, Jesus's own family of disciples. This part of Scripture does not even touch on forgiveness outside the community, important as that is. Why this careful attention to the dynamics of relationship and power in the church? Because transgressions happen. *Forgive us our trespasses as we forgive those who trespass against us.*

There is yet another passage, unique to Matthew's Gospel, in which Jesus takes the dynamics of forgiveness and reconciliation even further. In the Sermon on the Mount, while warning against anger toward a fellow disciple, Jesus makes his point in dramatic terms. "Therefore, if you are offering your gift at the altar"—this can only mean the altar in the Jerusalem temple—"and there remember that your brother or sister has something against you, leave your gift there in front of the altar. First go and be reconciled to them; then come and offer your gift" (5:23–24). In this decidedly Jewish illustration, Jesus is teaching his disciples somewhere in Galilee, probably eighty miles or so from Jerusalem. His disciples must imagine having made the considerable trek from Galilee all the way into the crowded streets of Jerusalem, gaining entry into the temple precinct, and finally approaching the altar with their sacrificial offering. "If you get there," Jesus says, "and remember that a fellow disciple *has something against you*, stop in your tracks. Go back—back the eighty or more miles into Galilee—find the person who harbors bad feelings toward you, and make it right. Be reconciled. Work it out. Then you can come back the eighty miles or so, all the way back to the temple, and offer your gift." And then return all the way home!

Perhaps Jesus is exaggerating in order to make a point, but that gives us a clue that his point is all the more important. Let us appreciate that Jesus places the priority on getting our relationships in order, setting things straight with one another, over offering our worship to God. This, we can confidently believe, is precisely what God desires. Jesus makes this explicit by quoting twice from the prophet Hosea, who is quoting God: "I desire mercy, not sacrifice" (Hosea 6:6; Matthew 9:13; 12:17). Mercy in this case is kindness and compassion toward others, while sacrifice is praise and worship toward God. God is neither so religious nor so self-absorbed as to prefer our praise over the hard labor of talking out our difficulties with one another.

It is also interesting that Jesus does not limit this instruction to our remembering that we have something against somebody else. Jesus says that, as I enter into the worship of God, if I suddenly recall that somebody else has something against *me*, God's will is that I go find that person and try to make it right. I might think that person is wrong. I might think I'm right. I might think they have no right to feel that way. I might be tempted simply to pass it off as their problem, not mine. I might think I will get around to it later—maybe even right after church. But Jesus says otherwise. "First go and be reconciled to them; then come and offer your gift."

I remember again my early days as a pastor. I had a family in the church whom I had felt for several weeks had been distant and cool toward me. I wasn't sure, but it was a feeling. One Sunday they missed both morning and evening services, and my concern grew. I remembered this passage from Matthew 5 and wondered whether, in fact, this key couple had something against me; if they did, I did not know what it might be. I decided to make a Sunday evening pastoral call, which was not my usual strategy! This was long before the days of cell phones, which likely would have made this whole escapade simpler. I think I decided not to call their home number ahead of time because it felt like an impromptu, face-to-face conversation was needed that would preclude complicated or anxious preparations. I decided just to go by and drop in, check on everybody, tell them we'd missed them in church, and see if anything further came to light.

As I drove up to their house, light did indeed become a factor. To be precise, just as I pulled up, their porch light went off. Oh. That didn't seem good. *Wow, what a way to welcome the pastor*, I thought. But I got out of the car, walked determinedly to the front door, and knocked with authority. I waited what seemed

*Even as the people of God,
we exist together in a
community where trespasses
and misunderstandings
are inevitable.*

like an appropriate amount of time, feeling snubbed by the doused light and the front door shut tight, then eventually walked away in a bit of a huff. Obviously, they *did* have something against me—and what a childish way to express it! I got in my car, turned the ignition, and began to pull away—just as the porch light came back on.

"Oh, wow!" I said, this time out loud. "Talk about immature behavior!" Now I was beginning to get angry. I drove around the neighborhood for a few minutes, trying to figure out what to do next. Jesus's words kept haunting me. My confidence was growing that someone had something against me. This assumption made me feel bad, of course, but I was also somewhat mystified since I did not know what the problem was. But I was feeling righteous! Here I had made the trip to their house, and they just turned the light off and on as a way to tell me I wasn't welcome! Well, I'd show them. I'd kill them with kindness if need be. I finally felt cooled down enough to circle back to their house.

As I drove up, the front porch light went off again. "You're kidding me," I said through clenched teeth, my stomach in knots. I pulled up, got out of the car, and banged hard on the front door with my fist. No matter what it was they were upset about, this was no way to act toward me, their pastor—or toward anyone else, for that matter. "I will not stand for this passive aggression," I muttered.

No reply at the door. I waited, now so confused as well as exasperated that I almost *hoped* no one would answer the door. Maybe I was making a mistake trying to force the issue. I waited another moment or two and then walked back, once more, to my car. I turned on the ignition once again and began to pull away from the curb—and, just then, the porch light came back on!

"Unbelievable!" I shouted to no one in particular. I think I shouted mostly to God. What should I do now?! What kind of strange and childish message were they sending with all this silly porch light stuff? Now I was getting really angry. All the more reason, I knew, that I should try one more time. I'm not good at rejection, and I like to be liked. This was not fun. But Jesus had taught us, his followers, to do the hard work of talking it out, seeking reconciliation, trying to understand, and getting past superficialities. I didn't drive around as long this time before I circled back again for a third try.

This time, the porch light was off. The after-dusk darkness was thickening, but there was sufficient ambient light to see the front door clearly. I strode with purpose to that front door and rang the doorbell, determined not to leave until someone opened up and spoke to me. I didn't have to wait long. The porch light came on again.

John* opened the door and stood in the doorway in his pajamas. "Pastor! Oh, man! Come in, come on in."

I was confused, taken aback, and not yet over my righteous indignation. But his welcome helped to put me a little more at ease.

"John, what's going on? I came by to see if you all were all right because we missed you in church today, and then all this turning lights on and off—what in the world?"

---

*Names have been changed.

"Oh, I know. Well, we're all sick. Everyone stayed in bed pretty much all day. And we had just turned off the lights inside, and the porch light too, to go to bed for the night. Sheila and I had just gotten into bed when we heard the knock on the door. I didn't get up right away because we've been having a lot of kids in the neighborhood lately pulling the old prank of knocking or ringing doorbells and running away. But when we heard it the second time, Sheila said maybe I should go check to see if someone was at the door. By the time I got out there and turned on the porch light, I looked out through the window and saw you driving away."

I wasn't sure whether I believed him. It seemed a little fishy.

"I waited a couple of minutes to give you time to get home," John continued, "and then called the parsonage. But nobody answered, so I left a message."

Of course, later that night, I did indeed hear John's recorded message. At the moment, though, I could only reply, "Well, I didn't go right home."

John continued, "Well, after I left the message, we weren't sure what to do but go back to bed. We're all just beat with this flu. So I turned off the porch light and went back to bed. Just about the time we were getting settled, we heard the door again. But we were feeling so lousy that I wasn't feeling much up to answering the door. It didn't really occur to me that it might be you again because I just assumed you'd gone home and by now probably heard my message. I thought this time it might be those neighbor kids. But when the bell rang again, I thought maybe I should get up and check. But with this fever I'm moving pretty slow, and by the time I got to the door and turned on the porch light again and looked out the window, there you were driving away again!

"So this time," John continued, "even though I turned off the light and went back to bed, I stayed a little more ready just in case you happened to show up one more time—and here you are!"

"Yes, here I am!"

Eventually, everyone got out of bed—John, Sheila, their three rambunctious boys, but not nearly so rambunctious this night because it was indeed obvious that everyone was sick. It turned into a wonderful pastoral call. I discovered, to my delight, that there really was nothing ominous between us (or at least nothing that was revealed!), that they had missed being in church, and that they all hoped to be back the following Sunday. I offered a prayer for healing for the entire family and left.

John eventually became one of my closest friends and confidants during our time with that congregation. I still look back on that evening as one on which I learned a couple of things: (1) sometimes circumstances nudge us to jump to conclusions, but it is best to be patient and withhold immediate judgment; and (2) the hard work of reconciliation is worth the effort.

Even as the people of God, we exist together in a community where trespasses and misunderstandings are inevitable. Maybe sometimes it will be merely a matter of bad timing. Often it will be something far more serious. Jesus instructs us through this prayer to acknowledge this fact, to realize that it means we will need to forgive, and to humbly admit that we will also need to be forgiven. We need to do the hard work of talking through our disagreements, hurts, disappointments, misunderstandings. We are only human, and we are human together. So we confess together, in prayer, *forgive us our trespasses as we forgive those who trespass against us.*

⚖ 6 ⚖

DELIVER US

And lead us not into temptation
But deliver us from evil
For yours is the kingdom and the power and the glory forever

Into Temptation

This part of the prayer can be troublesome, raising a theological quandary or two. Why would Jesus teach us to ask God not to lead us into temptation? That sounds so far from God's character, especially when we consider how bluntly James puts it in his epistle: "When tempted, no one should say, 'God is tempting me.' For God cannot be tempted by evil, nor does he tempt anyone" (1:13). That would seem to put the matter to rest. So what are we praying when we pray, "Lead us not into temptation"?

It may help to consider other translations of the text. The New Revised Standard Version (NRSV) reads, "And do not bring us to the time of trial, but rescue us from the evil one" (Matthew 6:13). Even here, however, the NRSV has a footnote indicating that "the time of trial" could also be translated "temptation," which returns us to our question: can God be associated with, or perhaps even blamed for, our struggles with temptation?

The ambiguity in this translation does provide an important key for attempting to answer this question. The key is this: in the Bible, there is a very fine line—if there is a line at all—between being tempted and being tested. The life of Jesus himself provides a compelling illustration. After his baptism, we read in Matthew, "Then Jesus was led by the Spirit into the wilderness to be tempted by the devil" (4:1). This period of temptation in the wilderness is clearly also a time of testing, just as the people of Israel are tested in the wilderness for forty years (Deuteronomy 8:2). We should note that Matthew links very closely the Holy Spirit's leading of Jesus and the devil's tempting of Jesus; the Spirit leads Jesus into the wilderness *for* this time of testing, trying, temptation. We might say God's Spirit is testing Jesus's mettle and that Satan is the agent of this testing. Strangely enough, the text seems to hint at a certain degree of collusion!

But perhaps this really isn't so strange. Recall the story of Job, in which the "angels came to present themselves before the LORD, and Satan [in Hebrew, *ha satan*, "the accuser"] also came with them to present himself before him" (2:1). There is no hint that this is unexpected or out of the ordinary; this accuser, or adversary, has a role to play in the divine court, something like a prosecuting attorney. (He is literally the devil's advocate!) Satan is there in the presence of God as loyal opposition. He challenges God's lofty estimation of Job—"no one on earth like him; he is blameless and upright, a man who fears God and shuns evil" (1:8; repeated verbatim in 2:3)—with the countering consideration that Job has had it awfully good. And we know the rest of the story.

It is noteworthy that, near the end of that story, when Job does gain an audience with God, the voice out of the whirlwind makes no mention of Satan or of the heavenly wager. (Remember, Satan is simply playing his designated role among the angels as the prosecutor.) God doesn't blame Satan for Job's misfortunes, as though the devil has sufficient power to threaten or even oppose God's purposes. Instead, God simply asks a series of questions to expose Job's utter ignorance: "Where were you when I laid the earth's foundation? Tell me, if you understand" (38:4). Creation is a vast, deep, and great mystery that infinitely transcends human understanding. In the book of Job, Satan is a servant of God who has a job to do within that mystery of creation. In this story, though Satan inflicts the testing of great loss and suffering upon Job, it all occurs under the auspices of the almighty God. Perhaps this sheds a little light on that strange petition, "Lead us not into temptation."

Interestingly, lest we assume that such an idea is unique to Job, there are hints of this understanding of Satan's role in the New Testament as well. In Luke 22, just before his arrest, Jesus says to Peter, "Simon, Simon, Satan has asked to sift all of you as wheat. But I have prayed for you, Simon, that your faith may not fail. And when you have turned back, strengthen your brothers" (vv. 31–32). The verb "asked" can also be translated as "obtained permission." This is a fascinating scenario: Jesus reports that Satan, the Adversary, has sought and received the go-ahead—much like the Job story—to test Jesus's disciples. Can there be any

"Lead us not into temptation"
is a prayer that acknowledges our
own weakness, our vulnerability,
and our fragility.

doubt regarding where permission was obtained? Satan is clearly assumed to be subservient to God. He is presented as the agent of testing and temptation, "to sift all of you as wheat." To sift wheat is to separate the good, edible grain from the useless chaff, and it is a necessary step in producing tasty, nourishing bread. Satan's role, while threatening, is ultimately beneficial—if, that is, one can endure the temptation and pass the test! Thus, Jesus assures Peter that he has prayed especially for Peter and that he will emerge from the time of trial to be a leader of Jesus's community.

The apostle Paul also contributes to our understanding of Satan, trials, temptations, and growth in Christian character. In 2 Corinthians 12, Paul, who is in the process of defending his apostolic authority to some Corinthian doubters, writes of "a person in Christ who fourteen years ago was caught up to the third heaven"—later he calls it "paradise"—and "heard things that are not to be told, that no mortal is permitted to repeat" (vv. 2, 4, NRSV). Context makes it abundantly clear that Paul is referring to himself. It's possible he is recalling his encounter with the risen Christ on the road to Damascus. In any case, Paul adds that, in light of "the exceptional character of the revelations," and "in order to keep me from becoming conceited, I was given a thorn in my flesh" (v. 7, NRSV and NIV). Of course, this thorn in the flesh has inspired many different guesses among Bible readers, but the point here is that the only thing Paul actually tells us about this thorn is that it is "a messenger of Satan to torment me, to keep me from being too elated" (v. 7, NRSV) about his unusually ecstatic religious experiences. Once again, Satan's role may include torment, and such torment is testing that could lead to temptation, but it is ultimately all in the interest of keeping Paul humble. "My grace is sufficient for you," Paul reports the Lord saying, "for my power is made perfect in weakness" (v. 9)—in this case, in Paul's weakness specifically associated with his "thorn in the flesh, a messenger of Satan."[1]

As a professor, I get to assume the role of test-giver. Certainly one purpose of a test is to determine the degree to which my students have understood and can recall what we have discussed in class. But any professor would agree that, to us, one of the greatest values of a test is that it encourages students to *study and try to learn* the material. Studying for a test, we hope, will help students better internalize those ideas that we most want to communicate. But, of course, there is no guarantee; a test can provide temptations as well, such as the temptation to blow it off or even perhaps to cheat. In these ways a test becomes an occasion for the testing of the student—not about ideas but about character. Indeed, sitting in a classroom, taking a test, and feeling the temptation to sneak a peek at a fellow student's answers is when a test becomes a temptation.

---

1. In this connection we might consider the two versions in the Bible of the story of David taking a census of his people, or at least of his armies. In 2 Samuel 24:1 we read that "the anger of the LORD burned against Israel, and he incited David against them, saying, 'Go and take a census of Israel and Judah.'" The commander of the armies, Joab, is hesitant to carry out the census because, in the words of commentary provided in *The Jewish Study Bible* (Oxford: Oxford University Press, 2004), "according to ancient belief counting people exposes them to misfortune (Ex. 30:11–16)" (p. 665). First Chronicles tells the same story but starts by stating that "Satan rose up against Israel and incited David to take a census of Israel" (21:1). Joab grudgingly obeys (vv. 3–4), and then God is described as "displeased with this thing" (v. 7, NRSV). There are undoubtedly historical and theological considerations that enter into this disparity in the stories, but this nonetheless provides a further example of the fascinating ambiguity in the Bible regarding Satan's role within the purview of God's providence.

Given these considerations, we might interpret the line, "Lead us not into temptation" to mean, "Do not give us tests that are so difficult they become temptations to quit." There is a note of realism here. Jesus definitely does not encourage us to a false bravado that might pray something like, "Testing? Bring it on!" Many scholars believe that the time of testing or temptation at the foreground of Jesus's mind is the coming siege and destruction of Jerusalem. This will be the ultimate testing for the Jewish people of the first century, including Jesus's own followers. Later in Matthew, Jesus tells his disciples, "When you see the desolating sacrilege standing in the holy place [the temple], . . . then those in Judea must flee to the mountains" (24:15–16, NRSV). This instruction makes no sense if Jesus is talking about the end of the world, and he isn't. He is, however, talking about the end of the world as the Jewish people know it—the end of Jerusalem, the destruction (again) of the temple, the dispersing of his fellow Jews under the might of the Roman army. This will be the great testing, a harrowing sifting of Israel.

Thus, Jesus continues, "How dreadful it will be in those days for pregnant women and nursing mothers!"—presumably because it is so much more difficult to flee or hide under those conditions, not to mention the extreme vulnerability of young lives (v. 19). "Pray that your flight will not take place in winter or on the Sabbath" (v. 20). These considerations are irrelevant if the entire world is coming to an end, but they are pertinent indeed if a severe testing is imminent. Arguably, Jesus's instructions to his disciples to pray, "Lead us not into temptation" fit perfectly into his words of warning in Matthew 24. This line in the Lord's Prayer might be understood roughly to be, "Deliver us, God, from the worst of the time of testing that is approaching."

The tests we face today presumably will be different—yet any time of testing in our lives has the potential to be difficult, stretching, painful, or harrowing. This line in the Lord's Prayer does not encourage us to actively seek such experiences. Later in the Sermon on the Mount, Jesus reminds us in another note of realism that "tomorrow will bring worries of its own. Today's trouble is enough for today" (6:34, NRSV). We ought not to bite off more than we can chew. "Lead us not into temptation" is a prayer that acknowledges our own weakness, our vulnerability, and our fragility. Thankfully, Scripture assures us that our Maker understands all of this. "As a father has compassion on his children, so the LORD has compassion on those who fear him; for he knows how we are formed; he remembers that we are dust" (Psalm 103:13–14).

When my wife, Janice, and I were much younger, we learned of various friends or parishioners undergoing terrible trials: the death of a child, a horrible, life-ending illness, car accidents, cancer—the list seems endless. It became our practice to say to each other, "We have never had to endure anything like this—but we will someday." It turned out we were right. Life has its way, sooner or later, of taking us all through times of severe testing, sorrow, and suffering. We need not go looking for experiences that will help us grow. "Lead us not into temptation."

Often, though not always, these times of testing and/or temptation are so intense, so deeply personal, that they are virtually impossible to share. There is no greater biblical example of this than the story of Abraham's offering of Isaac.

*Even as we revel in the reality
that we are God's children
through Jesus, we remember
that we are finite and frail
creatures of dust.*

This is how the story begins: "Some time later God tested Abraham" (Genesis 22:1). Why such a test as this? "Take your son, your only son, whom you love—Isaac—and go to the region of Moriah. Sacrifice him there as a burnt offering on a mountain I will show you" (v. 2). We know the rest of the story. But let us ask a question that the Jewish tradition has raised for centuries: Where is Sarah in all of this? Does she know? Does Abraham tell her? *Can* he tell her what happened on that mountain? Does Isaac ever tell his mother what happened on that mountain? Can Isaac ever look at his aged father in the same way again, after this? And if Sarah does learn what happened up there on Mount Moriah, how can she look at her husband through all the days of the rest of their lives together? How does this horrific moment impact their relationship? Will she—can she—ever believe Abraham that God gave this command and then reversed it?[2]

What a terrible testing of Abraham. Today, of course, if someone were to claim that God demanded the sacrifice of one of their children, we would rightly institutionalize such a person and get them on medication immediately. But the Bible teaches us that, for Abraham, this really is a test from God. What Jesus teaches us to pray is for easier tests. Need I add that there is nothing wrong with that?

Kingdom, Power, Glory

We end the prayer that Jesus has taught us to pray by reaffirming, confessing once more, that this is not about us. It is not our kingdom, power, or glory. Even as we rejoice that, through

---

2. The classic engagement with this story from within the Christian tradition remains the Danish philosopher Soren Kierkegaard's *Fear and Trembling*.

Jesus Christ, we can boldly approach the throne of grace and cry, *"Abba!"* we remember that it is not our throne but God's. Even as we revel in the reality that we are God's children through Jesus, we remember that we are finite and frail creatures of dust. The God of all creation is the one to whom we lift up our hearts, our praise, our gratitude, our very lives.

The God we worship, however, is no egomaniac. God is not a power-hungry ogre, nor an insecure, cosmic bully in need of constant obeisance. We believe and confess that God is love (1 John 4:8, 16)—self-giving, other-receiving, outpouring, and nurturing love for all creatures in the unimaginably vast entirety of creation. We exist on our beautiful planet within one mind-blowingly large galaxy that is but one of millions, probably billions, of galaxies. How do we even begin to wrap our minds around this? But when we pray, we address ourselves to the Creator, Sustainer, and Lover of it all. *To you belong the kingdom and the power and the glory forever.*

The God we worship does not hoard this power, does not selfishly grasp for glory, does not clench the kingdom in tight-fisted omnipotence. We know this because of Jesus. When Jesus invites us, "Come to me, all you who are weary and burdened, and I will give you rest. Take my yoke upon you and learn from me, for I am gentle and humble in heart, and you will find rest for your souls" (Matthew 11:28–29), it is the very voice of God, the very invitation of God, that we hear. The Father whom Jesus reveals (11:27) is *gentle and humble in heart.* Such love, such wondrous love!

The God we worship is a sharing and outpouring God. We know this because of Jesus, and we know it also because of what God has done *for* Jesus. God raised Jesus from the dead, and it is that risen Jesus who said to his astounded disciples, "All authority in heaven and on earth has been given to me" (Matthew 28:18). The passive verb "has been given" denotes the activity of God. God, whom Jesus describes in a prayer as "Lord of heaven and earth" (Matthew 11:25), has given Jesus God's authority in heaven and on earth. The language here is highly reminiscent of Daniel 7, where the prophet describes his vision in the night:

> *As I looked, thrones were set in place, and the Ancient of Days took his seat. His clothing was as white as snow; the hair of his head was white like wool. His throne was flaming with fire, and its wheels were all ablaze. (v. 9)*

> *In my vision at night I looked, and there before me was one like a son of man, coming with the clouds of heaven. He approached the Ancient of Days and was led into his presence. He was given authority, glory and sovereign power; all nations and peoples of every language worshiped him. His dominion is an everlasting dominion that will not pass away, and his kingdom is one that will never be destroyed. (vv. 13–14)*

The giving of all dominion, power, and glory from God (the Ancient of Days) to a "son of man" (a human) is a vision fulfilled in the resurrection and glorification of the crucified Nazarene, Jesus. Note that Daniel foresees that "all nations and peoples of every language worshipped him," which corresponds perfectly with Jesus's Great Commission: "Therefore go and make disciples of all nations" (Matthew 28:19).

But it is important to appreciate the nature of this dominion. While Jesus has received "all authority in heaven and on earth," he does not wield this authority in a domineering or coercive way. He is gentle and humble in heart, the very unveiling of God's heart of gentle love toward all creation. Thus, he does not exercise his divine power to force the nations into the reign of God: this would be precisely contrary to the nature of God! Instead, having received all divine authority, Jesus says, "*Therefore* go and make disciples of all nations, baptizing them in the name of the Father and of the Son and of the Holy Spirit, and teaching them to obey everything I have commanded you" (28:19–20a). The nature of this divine power and authority is expressed in the sending of his disciples not to conquer, not to force people, but to *teach* all the people "everything I have commanded you." It is precisely in this way that Jesus's dominion over all the peoples of the earth is to be expressed. Let us recall just a sampling of those teachings:

"Blessed are the peacemakers, for they will be called children of God." (Matthew 5:9)

In the same way, let your light shine before others, that they may see your good deeds and glorify your Father in heaven." (5:16)

"Leave your gift there in front of the altar. First go and be reconciled to them; then come and offer your gift." (5:24)

"If anyone forces you to go one mile, go with them two miles." (5:41)

"But I tell you, love your enemies and pray for those who persecute you, that you may be children of your Father in heaven. He causes his sun to rise on the evil and the good, and sends rain on the righteous and the unrighteous." (5:44–45)

"Not everyone who says to me, 'Lord, Lord,' will enter the kingdom of heaven, but only the one who does the will of my Father who is in heaven." (7:21)

"But go and learn what this means: 'I desire mercy, not sacrifice.' For I have not come to call the righteous, but sinners." (9:13)

If you had known what these words mean, 'I desire mercy, not sacrifice,' you would not have condemned the innocent." (12:7)

Jesus replied, "They do not need to go away. You give them something to eat." (14:16)

Then Jesus said to his disciples, "Whoever wants to be my disciple must deny themselves and take up their cross and follow me." (16:24)

"Therefore, whoever takes the lowly position of this child is the greatest in the kingdom of heaven. And whoever welcomes one such child in my name welcomes me." (18:4–5)

What an upside-down kingdom! What strange power! What humble glory! And Jesus demonstrates this power and authority by relying on his disciples—folks like you and me—to go out and teach these things, to make fellow disciples, to bring new people into this community of Jesus followers through the rite of baptism. This is not baptism by the sword but by the word of gentleness, of humility, of kindness, of mercy (Matthew 12:18–21). It is the word of invitation: "Come to me, all you who are weary and burdened, and I will give you rest. Take my yoke upon you and learn from me, for I am gentle and humble in heart, and you will find rest for your souls. For my yoke is easy and my burden is light" (11:28–30).

This is the sort of kingdom, power, and glory our God has and has generously shared with the risen Son, Jesus. And that risen Son—yesterday, today, and forever—is gentle and humble in heart. That is the nature of the kingdom into which you and I are invited when we pray the Lord's Prayer together.

AFTERWORD
IN JESUS'S NAME?

————◆◆◆————

What does it mean to pray "in Jesus's name," and why do we do it? If it is not simply a pious addendum to tack on at the end—a quick *in-Jesus's-name-amen*—what is its purpose?

First, it is helpful to note that the specific instruction to pray in Jesus's name is unique to the Gospel of John, but it appears there several times:

> *"And I will do whatever you ask in my name, so that the Father may be glorified in the Son. You may ask me for anything in my name, and I will do it." (John 14:13–14)*

> *"You did not choose me, but I chose you and appointed you so that you might go and bear fruit—fruit that will last—and so that whatever you ask in my name the Father will give you." (15:16)*

> *"In that day you will no longer ask me anything. Very truly I tell you, my Father will give you whatever you ask in my name. Un-*

til now you have not asked for anything in my name. Ask and you will receive, and your joy will be complete." (16:23–24)

"In that day you will ask in my name. I am not saying that I will ask the Father on your behalf. No, the Father himself loves you because you have loved me and have believed that I came from God." (16:26–27)

Since this specific formulation of asking the Father in Jesus's name is unique to John, it should not be surprising that the Lord's Prayer—found not in John's Gospel but only in Matthew and Luke—does not conclude with, "In Jesus's name, Amen." We will return to this consideration a little later. For the moment, let us return to our question: what does it mean to pray in Jesus's name?

Two considerations immediately suggest themselves. The first is that, when we pray in Jesus's name, we are acknowledging the fact that we are not approaching God in prayer on our own merits, or because we thought it was a good idea. We are praying precisely *because of Jesus*. This is especially important in New Testament theology because the mystery of Christ (Ephesians 1:9; 3:4–6)—truly revolutionary in the first century—is that non-Jewish peoples are being invited into the presence of the living God of Israel. We "who once were far away" (Ephesians 2:13) from the God of Abraham and Sarah, of Isaac and Rebekah, of Jacob and Leah and Rachel, we who were "without hope and without God in the world" (v. 12) have been brought near to the God of "the covenants of the promise" (v. 12) by way of the life, death, and resurrection of Jesus. We who are not of the people Israel may now boldly approach the God of Israel, the God revealed in the history and religious devotion of Israel—because of Jesus and in his name.

To pray in Jesus's name, then, is to acknowledge from the heart that we do not stand on ground that we ourselves carved out. We do not stand before God on our own merits or virtue or initiative. God has taken the initiative, in Jesus, to create a ground on which we may stand in prayer. So when we pray, we pray *through* Jesus. That ground for our praying includes the garden of Gethsemane, the foot of the cross, and the empty tomb. Paul repeatedly makes this point in his letters:

> *"For no matter how many promises God has made, they are 'Yes' in Christ. And so through him the 'Amen' is spoken by us to the glory of God." (2 Corinthians 1:20)*

> *"Such confidence we have through Christ before God." (2 Corinthians 3:4)*

> *"For through him [Christ] we both [Jew and gentile] have access to the Father by one Spirit." (Ephesians 2:18)*

> *"And whatever you do, whether in word or deed, do it all in the name of the Lord Jesus, giving thanks to God the Father through him." (Colossians 3:17)*

To put it most simply and obviously, we do not approach God in our own name but in Jesus's name. He has cleared the ground upon which we stand in prayer to the One he called—and invites us to call—*Abba*.

The second consideration is that, when we pray in Jesus's name, we are consciously attempting to align our hearts with the

Spirit of Jesus's own prayer life, "who calls out, *'Abba*, Father'" (Galatians 4:6). To pray in Jesus's name is to pray as Jesus prays— most particularly when he prays in Gethsemane, *"Abba*, Father . . . yet not what I will, but what you will" (Mark 14:36). We have mentioned already, of course, that Jesus has explicitly taught us to pray the same thing: "Your kingdom come, your will be done on earth"—in me—"as it is in heaven." So to pray in Jesus's name is to make his own prayer our own. Jesus has never prayed self-ish, grasping prayers. The one who prays from his cross, "Father, forgive them, for they do not know what they are doing" (Luke 23:34) continues even now to make intercession for us (Hebrews 7:25) and for all.

Paul writes, "The death he died, he died to sin once for all; but the life he lives, he lives to God" (Romans 6:10). The resur-rected Jesus lives *to* God, *for* God, and *in the presence of* God on our behalf (Romans 8:34). To pray in Jesus's name is to pray in the same spirit as Jesus prays, in self-emptying love—and that spirit is the Holy Spirit. Thus, the New Testament generally encourages us toward worship and prayer *to* the Father, *through* Jesus the Son, *in* the Spirit (Ephesians 2:18). This is the Trinitarian form and logic of Christian prayer, especially as described by Paul.

Sadly this Trinitarian logic is often ignored or misunder-stood. Hence, we often hear prayers addressed to Jesus that end with "in Jesus's name" or "in your name." Surely we perceive the oddity of praying *to* Jesus *in* Jesus's name. John Wesley even warned specifically in *A Plain Account of Christian Perfection*, "Do not direct your prayers to Christ only, without either having or seeking to have access to the Father through him."[1] Alternatively, it is not unusual to hear prayers addressed to "our Father" that end with, "We pray in your name." Again, this misses the point. We have been invited to approach God in worship, praise, and prayer through Jesus Christ, so we pray specifically in Jesus's name. A thoroughly Christian understanding of prayer is that we pray:

- *in* the Spirit—that is, empowered and enabled by God's own Spirit to pray (Romans 8:26–27);
- *through* the Son—that is, in his name and by virtue of what he has accomplished for us through his ministry, crucifixion, and resurrection (Ephesians 2:12–18);
- *to* the Father, who sent forth his Son into the world and the Spirit of his Son into our hearts in order to draw us into the blessedness of eternal fellowship (Galatians 4:4–6; 2 Corinthians 1:21–22).

Wesley wrote, accordingly, "The whole Trinity is engaged in our redemption; each of the sacred Persons bears some peculiar office, and has blessings for all who draw nigh in full assurance of faith."[2]

Wesley also went on to concede that "these are comparatively small things,"[3] and so it might seem. Leave it to theologians to get nitpicky about how we conclude our prayers! But there is an important consideration here. When we pray—especially when we pray publicly, in church, or in positions of church leadership—we are being called upon to pray intelligently and coherently within a community of faith that has a specific history and identity. We're

---

1. Wesley, *A Plain Account*, 138.
2. Wesley, *A Plain Account*, 138.
3. Wesley, *A Plain Account*, 138.

not just praying in general to a generalized God. We are confessing our identity as God's children, forgiven and adopted by divine grace that has been lavished upon us through Jesus Christ and actualized in our hearts and lives by the life-giving, transforming presence of the Spirit. It never hurts a congregation to hear this in prayer, or to be informed by such prayer. While prayer is primarily addressed to God, it is also an opportunity to teach God's people: this prayer addressed to God is offered up in Jesus's name and in the confidence that this prayer is offered in the power and presence of the Spirit, who is the initiator and enlivener of all truly Christian praying.

When we pray to Jesus "in Jesus's name" or pray to the Father "in your name," we are risking a gross misunderstanding of the very (theo)logic of Christian prayer. It is not that God cannot or will not hear such prayers—we are not talking about magical passwords to get God's attention—but that we are impoverishing Christian faith, practice, and community when we ignore or violate the Trinitarian pattern of prayer. Praying to God apart from Jesus's name (for example, a prayer that ends simply with "Amen") implies that we address a solitary deity rather than the profoundly social God of triune faith and confession. A solitary deity corresponds all too nicely with individualistic, solitary religiosity—"the flight of the alone to the Alone," as the ancient philosopher Plotinus famously put it. But, as Wesley insisted, Christianity is a social religion, so it is no surprise that the social reality of Christianity (the church) prays to the triune God, whose social nature, while incomprehensible, is undeniable. So we pray *in* the Spirit *through* the Son *to* the Father, and confess that this Spirit-Son-Father is, mysteriously, *all truly God*. We pray in God, through God, to God. God is love: the infinite mystery of self-giving, other-receiving, eternally nurturing relations.

Occasionally, ministers who have come to appreciate this Trinitarian vision of God use a different ending for public prayers: "in the name of the Father and of the Son and of the Holy Spirit. Amen." At the risk of sounding terribly touchy about this, let me insist that this also is a misunderstanding of Christian prayer. We are not praying in the name of Father, Son, and Spirit; we are praying *to* the Father *in the name of* the Son *in the power of* the Spirit. Yes, we baptize people "in the name of the Father and of the Son and of the Holy Spirit" (Matthew 28:19), but that is not prayer. A minister may offer a benediction at the end of a worship service "in the name of the Father and of the Son and of the Holy Spirit"—but a benediction is also not prayer. It is the bestowal of a blessing upon the people.

In the Lord's Prayer, Jesus has taught us to pray to our Father in heaven. There is little in the New Testament that encourages prayer to Jesus, though undoubtedly those prayers often come naturally enough. There certainly are times when "Dear Jesus!" just seems like the right prayer, and I truly doubt this causes rumbles in the Trinity! But as Christians, we are Trinitarians, and our public and ecclesial prayers should especially reflect this. On this subject Wesley wrote further, "Indeed in the infant state of our conversion it is usual to have an intercourse with the Son of God only. . . . But as faith increases, the door in heaven is opened wider, the veil further rent away; and perfect faith will display the undivided Three-in-One . . . the whole, triune God."[4]

---

4. Wesley, *A Plain Account*, 138.

To return to our initial question, why do we not end the Lord's Prayer with the phrase, "In Jesus's name, Amen"? The simple reply is that neither Matthew nor Mark tells us that Jesus says we should. However—and this is an extremely important point—Jesus has taught us, his disciples, to pray this prayer, and without Jesus we would not be praying this (or any) prayer to the God of Israel. We cannot help but pray this prayer in Jesus's name, even if we never explicitly say it. But it is good to say so. The way I came to incorporate the Lord's Prayer into the weekly Sunday morning worship services where I was appointed as interim pastor was to make it the conclusion of the pastoral prayer. There is a beautiful way to make a seamless transition from the pastoral prayer to the Lord's Prayer, along these lines: *We pray all these things in the name of Jesus Christ our Lord, who has taught us to pray.* . . . This transition line also functions as an invitation to the congregation to join the pastor in reciting the Lord's Prayer together.

My only prayer, here in the concluding words of this little collection of meditations on the Lord's Prayer, is that this book will help us pray this beautiful prayer like we mean it. *In Jesus's holy name, Amen.*